*THE*

# GRACIAS MADRE
-COOKBOOK-

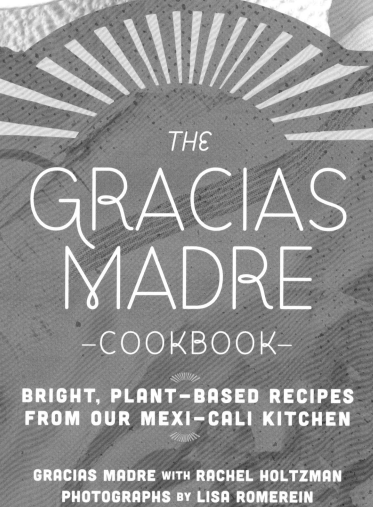

# THE GRACIAS MADRE

# COOKBOOK

## BRIGHT, PLANT-BASED RECIPES FROM OUR MEXI-CALI KITCHEN

GRACIAS MADRE WITH RACHEL HOLTZMAN
PHOTOGRAPHS BY LISA ROMEREIN

AVERY
AN IMPRINT OF PENGUIN RANDOM HOUSE
NEW YORK

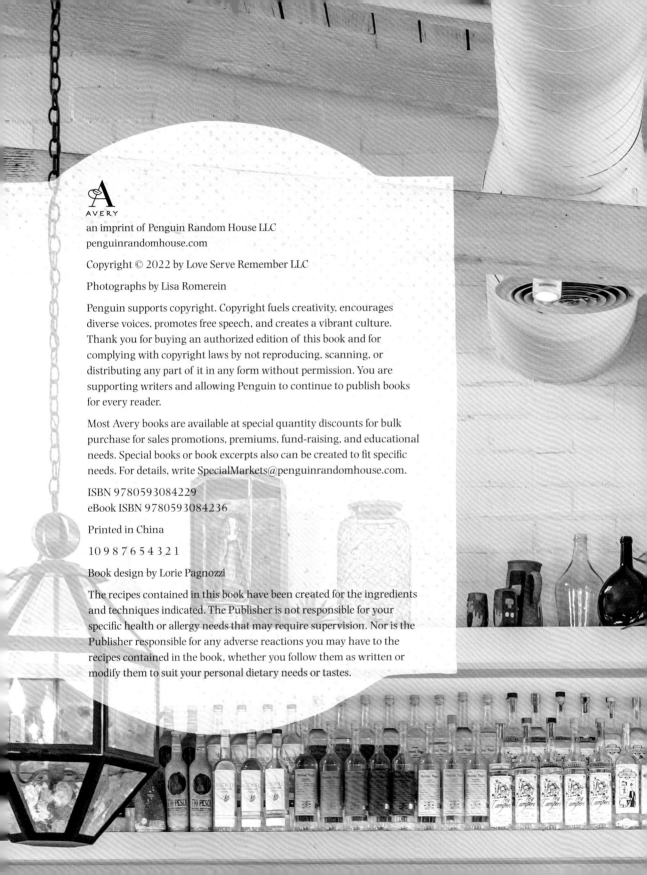

A
AVERY

an imprint of Penguin Random House LLC
penguinrandomhouse.com

Most Avery books are available at special quantity discounts for bulk purchase for sales promotions, premiums, fund-raising, and educational needs. Special books or book excerpts also can be created to fit specific needs. For details, write SpecialMarkets@penguinrandomhouse.com.

ISBN 9780593084229
eBook ISBN 9780593084236

Printed in China

10 9 8 7 6 5 4 3 2 1

Book design by Lorie Pagnozzi

This book is dedicated to our staff, our farmers, and our cherished guests. We will forever be grateful for your support; we are more vibrant today because of you.

# CONTENTS

# INTRODUCTION

I t's no surprise that Gracias Madre, as the sister restaurant to Café Gratitude, has its roots in saying "Thank you." Our highest calling has always been in service to our community, giving people fresh food made with integrity from ingredients grown with love. So when our founding chef, Chandra Gilbert—who was then the executive chef at the original Café Gratitude in San Francisco—noticed that their employees were slinking out to taquerías in the Mission District for lunch (as most people do to get their fix of great Mexican food), we knew that there was more we could be doing—both in providing the most nourishing, nutritious food for the people who graced us with their hard work and in giving our wider community the gift of equally delicious but decidedly plant-based and organic Mexican food.

Around that same time, our founders, Terces and Matthew Engelhart, had been visiting the villages of our employees all over Mexico—Hidalgo, Jallsco, Oxkutzcab, Oaxaca, Chihuahua, Yucatán. What they received there were unparalleled warmth and hospitality, along with no shortage of delicious home-cooked meals. Born from those trips was the idea that our next endeavor should be dedicated to the same big-hearted spirit that was demonstrated around those tables—the generosity of the mother, who regularly sacrifices comfort and rest in the name of her family, and the spirit of Our Lady of Guadalupe, the ultimate provider and nourisher of souls, whose image adorned the mantels and altars in many of the homes the Engelharts visited. To them we wanted to say, "Thank you, Mother," or *Gracias Madre*.

And so, in the mother's name, we created a restaurant that celebrates the culinary traditions of Mexico, with a fresh California twist. Just as we had with Café Gratitude—to an enormously positive response—we wanted to offer our guests dishes that didn't apologize for being plant-based. Quite the opposite: These are dishes that rejoice in their connection to the land and call forth flavor, substance, tradition, and joy in abundance. It makes sense—Mexican food is, in many ways, one of the original vegan cuisines. Before the Spanish conquistadores brought with them new ingredients, including many dairy products, the Mexican pantry centered around what's called "The Three Sisters" in Mesoamerican culture: beans, corn, and chiles. (Squash also plays a very important role in the ecosystem, but those three are always the leads.) By embracing these workhorses, layering in chile- and spice-filled salsas and moles, and experimenting with creative whole-food twists on traditional meat fillings (mushroom carnitas and al pastor, jackfruit mixiote, dehydrated hibiscus) as well as nut-based cheeses (cashew crema and queso blanco, almond cotija), we have created a menu filled with well-loved Cali-Mexican classics.

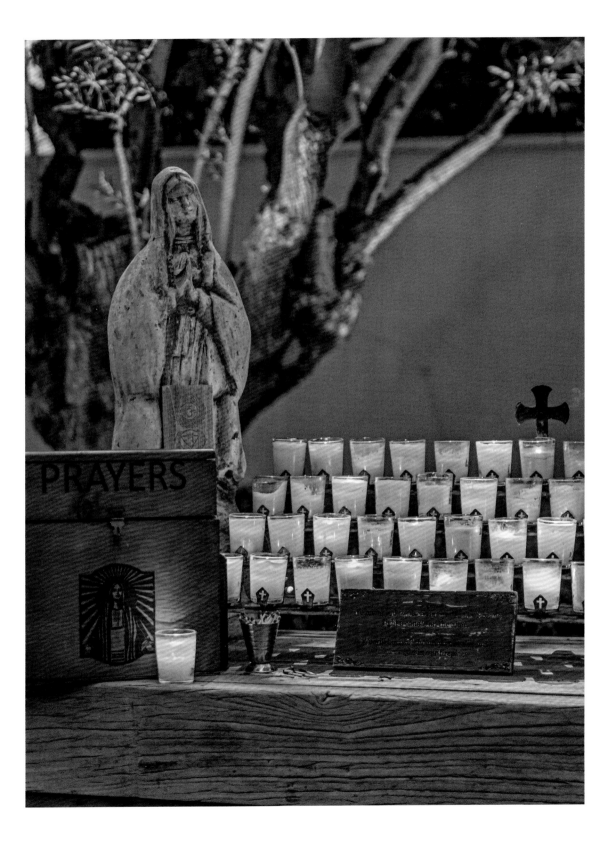

When it came time to follow in the footsteps of Gratitude and bring Gracias Madre from San Francisco to Los Angeles, we knew that we wanted to once again put our signature Love Serve Remember stamp on the concept. While still preserving the namesake open-arms hospitality and commitment to high-quality food, we also wanted to give our guests a sensual space for meeting, eating, and sharing a great signature cocktail—which has earned the name "Sexican"—whether for a light lunch of baby coconut ceviche and pozole; an all-out fiesta with an endless spread of esquites, flautas, tacos, gorditas, and enchiladas; or just a dinner out of our famous guacamole and a few rounds of tequila palomas.

Over time, we've realized that what we've created is special. It really has been a blended effort, from Chandra's original vision, to the Engelharts' graciousness of spirit, to our team's contributions of heirloom recipes and techniques from their own families, to the design and vision of Lisa Bonbright and Love Serve Remember, and to the preservation of tradition—while also evolving into the future, thanks to Gracias Madre's most recent chef, Alan Sánchez, who was with us from 2019 to 2021. This restaurant is a place that makes our guests feel cared for and nurtured without sacrificing style or fun, and continues to make good on our original intention to give our gratitude to the men and women who have helped build this business. The Gracias Madre community is one that supports from within, creating opportunities and experiences for those who come to us with few or little of either. And in the kitchen, we give back to our passionate cooks by providing an education in the anatomy of Mexican food, spirits, flavors, and techniques.

And now we want to share that love with you. With these recipes, you'll be able to re-create our fresh, inspired dishes in your own kitchen. There may be some ingredients you haven't worked with before (nothing you can't find in your local Mexican market or online!), and there may be some techniques that are new to you (like folding tamales or making your own tortillas), but at the heart of this book are simple recipes that bring fresh, organic ingredients to life.

# CHAPTER 1

# STARTERS

# TOSTADAS

Most people know that Mexico has a rich street-food culture, but what they don't often realize is that there's nuance to these dishes—particularly as to when they're offered. Depending on the time of day (morning, noon, evening, and late night), you'll see different types of street food on display. Late at night, for example, when people are pouring out of the bars, little carts pull up and people open their garages to sell their tostadas. The anatomy of a tostada is simple: a fried (or sometimes baked) tortilla loaded with beans, cream, and then all kinds of toppings depending on where in the country you are. In the north of Mexico, it's common to find them mounded with seafood, which is the inspiration for our coconut ceviche version. In central Mexico, tostadas get topped with pit-barbecued meat, or mixiote—which we re-create using pulled jackfruit smothered in a salsa ranchera–spiked barbecue sauce. And in many regions, you'll often see these topped with mushrooms, which we also offer, spiced with guajillo chiles and heaped on a base of creamy chipotle hummus.

## TOSTADAS AL AJILLO

SERVES 4

### FOR THE CHIPOTLE HUMMUS

1 (15-ounce) can chickpeas, drained and liquid reserved

⅓ cup fresh lime juice

¼ cup tahini

¼ cup extra-virgin olive oil

1 small chipotle in adobo

1 garlic clove

½ teaspoon ground cumin

¼ teaspoon chipotle powder

¼ teaspoon Himalayan salt

(INGREDIENTS AND RECIPE CONTINUE)

## FOR THE AJILLO MUSHROOMS

4 dried guajillo chiles, stemmed and seeded

¼ cup extra-virgin olive oil

4 garlic cloves, minced

6 cups sliced cremini mushrooms

¾ teaspoon Himalayan salt

## FOR THE ROASTED CHERRY TOMATOES

15 cherry tomatoes, halved

2 teaspoons extra-virgin olive oil

½ teaspoon fresh thyme leaves

¼ teaspoon Himalayan salt

## FOR ASSEMBLY

Canola, rice bran, or other neutral oil, for frying

4 Tortillas (page 209), or store-bought corn tortillas

½ cup fresh sorrel, cilantro, or parsley leaves

Lemon wedges

**MAKE THE CHIPOTLE HUMMUS:** In a high-speed blender, add the chickpeas, lime juice, tahini, olive oil, chipotle in adobo, garlic, cumin, chipotle powder, and salt. Blend until smooth. If needed, add a tablespoon or two of the reserved chickpea liquid to loosen up the hummus. Taste and adjust the seasoning.

**MAKE THE MUSHROOMS:** In a medium bowl, add the guajillos with enough hot water to cover. Soak until the chiles have softened, about 15 minutes. Drain and chop the chiles.

In a large nonstick or cast-iron pan over medium-high heat, heat the olive oil. Add the garlic and cook just until fragrant, about 1 minute. Add the mushrooms and guajillos and cook, stirring, until the mushrooms are tender, 5 to 7 minutes. Add the salt and cook for 2 more minutes.

**MAKE THE CHERRY TOMATOES:** Preheat the oven to 400°F. Line a baking sheet with parchment.

In a medium bowl, add the cherry tomatoes, olive oil, thyme, and salt and toss to coat. Spread the tomatoes out onto a baking sheet and roast for 15 minutes.

In a heavy-bottomed, high-sided frying pan over medium-high heat, heat about 1 inch of canola oil to 350°F. Line a plate or baking sheet with a few layers of paper towels and place nearby for draining.

Fry the tortillas in the hot oil until golden, 1 to 2 minutes per side. Transfer to the plate to drain and repeat with the remaining tortillas.

Spread each tostada with about ¼ cup of the hummus. Divide the ajillo mushrooms evenly among the tostadas and top with the roasted cherry tomatoes. Garnish with the fresh herbs and serve with lemon wedges.

# TOSTADAS AL CEVICHE

SERVES 4

Canola, rice bran, or other neutral oil, for frying

4 Tortillas (page 209), or store-bought corn tortillas

⅔ cup Guacamole (page 41)

1 recipe Madre Coconut Ceviche (page 27)

1 watermelon radish, thinly sliced

1 Persian cucumber, thinly sliced

1 serrano chile, seeded and thinly sliced (optional)

¼ cup chopped fresh cilantro

In a heavy-bottomed, high-sided frying pan over medium-high heat, heat about 1 inch of oil to 350°F. Line a plate or baking sheet with a few layers of paper towels and place nearby for draining.

Fry the tortillas in the hot oil until golden, 1 to 2 minutes per side. Transfer to the plate to drain and repeat with the remaining tortillas.

Spread the tostadas with the guacamole, then a layer of the ceviche. Garnish with the radish, cucumber, and the serrano chile, if using. Finish with the cilantro.

# TOSTADAS AL JACKFRUIT MIXIOTE

SERVES 4

Canola, rice bran, or other neutral oil, for frying

1 small onion, thinly sliced, rings broken up

Himalayan salt, to taste

4 Tortillas (page 209), or store-bought corn tortillas

1 cup Black Beans (page 221)

2 cups Jackfruit Mixiote (page 211)

½ cup Cashew Crema (page 184)

¼ cup chopped fresh cilantro

In a heavy-bottomed, high-sided frying pan over medium-high heat, heat about 1 inch of oil to 350°F. Line a plate or baking sheet with a few layers of paper towels and place nearby for draining.

Add the sliced onions to the oil and fry until just golden, about 1 minute. Transfer to the plate to drain and season immediately with a pinch of salt.

Fry the tortillas in the hot oil until golden, 1 to 2 minutes per side. Transfer to the plate to drain and repeat with the remaining tortillas.

Spread the tostadas with a thin layer of the black beans and top with the jackfruit. Finish with the crispy fried onions, cashew crema, and cilantro.

# BUTTERNUT SQUASH TAQUITOS

You may know taquitos as a freezer aisle staple that you sometimes microwaved after school, but in Mexico, they're a snack that we make fresh or buy from street vendors at night. They show up pretty regularly in our day-to-day, mostly as an accompaniment to other dishes—particularly pozole, which is typically offered up wherever you find taquitos. You can fill these with practically anything, but we like crispy butternut squash, a take on traditional Mexican squash fillings but updated with caramelized onions and meaty hemp seeds.

MAKES 16 TAQUITOS

1 medium butternut squash, cut in half lengthwise and seeds removed

1 tablespoon extra-virgin olive oil

1 medium onion, thinly sliced

1½ teaspoons Himalayan salt

5 garlic cloves, chopped

¼ cup hemp seeds, toasted

1 tablespoon paprika

1 tablespoon ground cumin

16 Tortillas (page 209), or store-bought corn tortillas, warmed and kept under a towel to stay soft

Canola, rice bran, or other neutral oil, for frying

Zest of 1 orange (optional)

2 cups Guacamole (page 41)

1 cup Cashew Crema (page 184)

1 cup Salsa Roja (page 190)

Preheat the oven to 350°F. Line a baking sheet with parchment.

Place the squash cut side down on the baking sheet and bake until the flesh is very soft and tender, about 1 hour.

(RECIPE CONTINUES)

In a large nonstick pan over medium-high heat, heat the olive oil. Add the onion and ½ teaspoon of the salt and cook, stirring occasionally, until the onions are translucent, 5 to 7 minutes. Reduce the heat to medium-low and continue cooking until the onions are deeply caramelized, 10 to 15 more minutes. Add the garlic and cook for 2 more minutes. Remove the pan from the heat and add the hemp seeds, paprika, cumin, and the remaining 1 teaspoon salt.

Scoop out the roasted squash from the skin into a large bowl. Discard the skin. Add the onion mixture and stir to combine. Taste and adjust the seasoning if needed.

Spread a few tablespoons of the squash mixture over each tortilla and carefully roll up the tortilla to form a cigar shape. Set the taquitos aside on a baking sheet as you assemble them.

In a heavy-bottomed, high-sided frying pan over medium-high heat, heat about 2 inches of canola oil to 350°F. Line a plate or baking sheet with a few layers of paper towels and place nearby for draining.

Using tongs, gently lay a few taquitos in the hot oil and fry until golden, 2 to 3 minutes per side. Transfer to the plate to drain. Repeat with the remaining taquitos. Top the just-fried taquitos with the orange zest, if using.

Serve with the guacamole, cashew crema, and salsa roja.

# STREET FRUIT

This fun, bright fruit salad with a spicy kick is a nod to the morning street vendors who come out offering selections of fresh fruit that they chop, then toss with lime juice, salt, and chili powder. We also add avocado (it's a fruit!) and coconut bacon for additional texture and body.

SERVES 4

2 cups cubed mango

2 cups cubed pineapple

2 cups strawberries, halved or
    quartered (depending on size)

Juice of 1 lime, plus additional
    lime wedges for serving

¼ teaspoon Himalayan salt,
    plus more to taste

1 avocado, cubed

½ cup Coconut Bacon
    (page 223)

Hot sauce, to taste

In a large bowl, add the mango, pineapple, strawberries, lime juice, and salt. Toss gently to combine. Add the avocado and toss once more. Taste and adjust seasoning if needed. Garnish with the coconut bacon, hot sauce, and lime wedges.

STREET FRUIT

# SALSA TRIO WITH HOMEMADE CHIPS

One of the defining features of great Mexican food is freshly made, as-spicy-as-you-can-handle salsas. Like most other traditional Mexican restaurants, we're big fans of starting off a meal with a selection of our house-made versions, which we serve with fresh tortilla chips. They're simple to re-create at home; they're always a crowd-pleaser; and you won't be mad at the leftovers, which you can mix and match with any dish in this book.

SERVES 8

## FOR THE PINEAPPLE HABANERO SALSA

1 habanero pepper

1 cup apple cider vinegar

1 teaspoon extra-virgin olive oil

1 cup diced onion

1 small garlic clove, minced

2½ cups diced fresh pineapple

½ cup sugar

1½ teaspoons chopped jalapeño

½ cup fresh lime juice

1 teaspoon Himalayan salt

## FOR THE MANGO SALSA

2 cups diced fresh mango

¼ cup diced red bell pepper

2 tablespoons fresh lime juice

2 tablespoons chopped fresh cilantro

1 tablespoon chopped fresh mint

1 tablespoon chopped fresh basil

1 tablespoon apple cider vinegar

1 teaspoon agave nectar

¼ to ½ jalapeño, seeded and minced (or leave seeds in for more heat)

¼ teaspoon Himalayan salt

## FOR THE TORTILLA CHIPS

Canola, rice bran, or other neutral oil, for frying

24 Tortillas (page 209), or store-bought corn tortillas, cut into quarters

Himalayan salt, to taste

## FOR SERVING

2 cups Pico de Gallo (page 194)

3 sprigs cilantro

**Make the pineapple salsa:** Preheat the oven to 350°F.

Place the habanero on a small baking sheet or piece of foil and roast for 10 minutes. Transfer to a high-speed blender, add the vinegar, and blend until smooth.

(RECIPE CONTINUES)

SALSA TRIO WITH HOMEMADE CHIPS

In a medium saucepan over medium heat, heat the olive oil. Add the onion and garlic and cook until the onion has just softened but not browned, about 5 minutes. Add the pineapple, sugar, jalapeño, and the vinegar mixture, increase the heat to high, and bring to a boil. Reduce the heat to low and simmer for 15 minutes. Add the lime juice and salt and simmer for 5 more minutes. Let cool completely before serving.

**Make the mango salsa:** In a medium bowl, add the mango, red pepper, lime juice, cilantro, mint, basil, vinegar, agave, jalapeño, and salt. Taste and adjust the seasoning.

**Make the tortilla chips:** In a Dutch oven, heavy-bottomed pot, or high-sided frying pan over medium-high heat, heat about 3 inches of canola oil to 350°F. Line a baking sheet with a few layers of paper towels and place nearby for draining.

Working in batches, fry the tortilla pieces until golden, 2 to 3 minutes, flipping occasionally to fry evenly. Transfer the chips to the baking sheet to drain and season immediately with salt. Repeat with the remaining tortilla pieces.

**Serve:** Place each salsa in a small bowl and garnish with the cilantro sprigs. Serve with the fresh chips.

# ESQUITES

In Mexico, you usually won't find this dish in a restaurant—unless it's a fancied-up version for fine dining—because it's such a street-food staple. Traditionally, it's anything *but* fancy, just corn, mayo, fresh cheese, lime, and chili powder. But since we like to give our guests something a cut above (without it being any less delicious and decadent), we've added a twist with our salsa verde alongside our cashew crema and almond cotija. Another noteworthy addition is fresh epazote, an herb native to Mexico that has an earthy flavor similar to oregano.

SERVES 4

3 cups corn, fresh or frozen and thawed

½ medium onion, chopped

2 sprigs fresh epazote

1 tablespoon Himalayan salt

2 tablespoons extra-virgin olive oil

1 cup Salsa Verde (page 191)

¼ cup Cashew Crema (page 184)

2 teaspoons Almond Cotija (page 183)

Pinch of chili powder

Lime wedges, for serving

In a large pot over medium-high heat, bring 6 cups of water to a boil. Add the corn, onion, epazote, and salt and cook until the corn is just tender, about 4 minutes. Drain and set aside.

In a large nonstick or cast-iron pan over medium-high heat, heat the olive oil. Add the corn and cook, stirring occasionally, until the corn begins to turn golden brown, 5 to 7 minutes. Add the salsa verde, bring to a simmer, and cook for 1 minute.

Divide the esquites among four bowls and finish with the cashew crema and almond cotija. Garnish with the chili powder and serve with the lime wedges.

# COLIFLOR FRITO

There's nothing traditionally Mexican about these crispy bits of cauliflower that have been smothered in nacho cheese—in fact, like nachos, they're a distinctly American invention—but no one's going to turn down a plate of these bites or argue that there's a better way to enjoy cauliflower.

SERVES 4

Canola, rice bran, or other neutral oil, for frying

5 cups cauliflower florets, cut into bite-size pieces

Himalayan salt, to taste

1 cup Cashew Nacho Cheese (page 181)

1 lemon, cut into wedges

In a Dutch oven, heavy-bottomed pot, or high-sided frying pan over high heat, heat about 3 inches of oil to 350°F. Line a baking sheet with a few layers of paper towels and place nearby for draining.

Working in batches so as not to crowd the pot, fry the cauliflower until golden, for 2 to 3 minutes, flipping the florets occasionally to fry evenly. Using a skimmer or slotted spoon, transfer the fried cauliflower to the baking sheet to drain and season immediately with salt. Repeat with the remaining cauliflower.

In a medium bowl, add the fried cauliflower with the nacho cheese and toss to coat. Transfer to a serving plate with the lemon wedges and a side of cheese sauce, if desired.

# FIDEO SECO

Mexican cooking includes influences from all over the world, including the ingredients Spaniards brought from Asia. Enter noodles into the ancestral Mexican kitchen. This dish, which takes those (gluten-free, vegan) noodles, fries them, tosses them with a tomato and chile sauce, and drizzles them with crema, is a homestyle mainstay.

SERVES 4

2 cups Salsa Ranchera (page 192)

1 chipotle in adobo

2 teaspoons extra-virgin olive oil

2 cups fideo pasta or vermicelli noodles, broken roughly into 2-inch pieces

2 cups boiling water

¼ cup Cashew Crema (page 184)

¼ cup chopped fresh cilantro

2 tablespoons Almond Cotija (page 183)

½ cup Guacamole (page 41)

In a high-speed blender, add the salsa ranchera and chipotle in adobo and blend until smooth.

In a large nonstick pan over medium heat, heat the oil. Add the fideos and toast, stirring frequently, until the pasta begins to turn golden, about 5 minutes. Add the salsa mixture and increase the heat to high, stirring constantly to help the pasta start to absorb the sauce. Bring to a simmer and reduce the heat to low. As you stir, add the boiling water, about ¼ cup at a time, turning and stirring until the water is absorbed. When the sauce begins to look dry again, repeat, adding the water in stages until the pasta is fully cooked, 10 to 15 minutes.

Divide the pasta among four plates and garnish with the cashew crema, cilantro, and almond cotija. Serve with the guacamole on the side.

# MADRE COCONUT CEVICHE

Ceviche is one of Mexico's most iconic dishes, thanks to the many states of the country that are close to the ocean and Gulf. Traditionally, it's made with fresh fish that's been "cooked" in the acid from fruits like passionfruit, lime, lemon, or grapefruit. So to make it our own, we use fresh young Thai coconut meat, which remarkably resembles the texture of fish, then add the sea vegetables nori and dulse to give the dish its signature from-the-sea flavor.

SERVES 4

2 cups shredded young Thai coconut, fresh or frozen, thawed and drained

¼ cup fresh lemon juice

¼ cup fresh lime juice

1 cup diced yellow squash

½ cup chopped fresh cilantro

¼ cup Pico de Gallo (page 194)

½ jalapeño, seeded and minced

½ sheet nori, finely crumbled

1 teaspoon dulse flakes or granules

1 teaspoon dried oregano

½ teaspoon Himalayan salt

¼ teaspoon freshly ground black pepper

### FOR SERVING

1 avocado, sliced

¼ cup fresh cilantro leaves

2 Persian cucumbers, thinly sliced

1 small watermelon radish, halved and thinly sliced

½ teaspoon smoked salt

**Make the ceviche:** Layer the coconut between two clean kitchen towels (or paper towels) and gently press down to dry the coconut thoroughly.

(RECIPE CONTINUES)

In a large bowl, add the coconut, lemon juice, and lime juice, and stir to combine. Cover and chill for about 1 hour to let the coconut marinate.

Add the squash, chopped cilantro, pico de gallo, jalapeño, nori, dulse, oregano, salt, and pepper. Stir gently to combine. Taste and adjust the seasoning.

**Serve:** Divide the ceviche among four bowls. Garnish with the avocado, cilantro leaves, cucumber, and radish. Finish with the smoked salt.

# MADRE CRAB CAKES

This mash-up dish is an homage to both the bar food classic as well as the seafood empanadas that you find at street carts and restaurants all over Mexico. We add a Mexican twist to the New England version by folding in fresh corn, and then of course put our Gracias Madre stamp on it by swapping out the crab for hearts of palm, which have a very similar texture. Serve these on their own as a tasty snack or starter, use them to top a bed of greens, or make a torta by sandwiching a couple of cakes between two slices of an aioli-slathered bolillo or other roll of your choice.

SERVES 4 (MAKES ABOUT 8 CAKES)

### FOR THE CRAB CAKES

1 tablespoon extra-virgin olive oil, plus more for frying

1 cup corn, fresh or frozen and thawed

2 teaspoons minced onion

2 teaspoons minced red bell pepper

4 whole hearts of palm, shredded (about 1 cup)

3 tablespoons panko breadcrumbs (gluten-free if desired), plus more for breading

1½ tablespoons vegan mayonnaise

1 tablespoon crushed nori

1 teaspoon chopped fresh parsley

½ teaspoon Old Bay seasoning

¼ teaspoon mustard powder

¼ teaspoon Himalayan salt

Pinch of freshly ground black pepper

### FOR SERVING

½ cup Spicy Mayo (page 177)

¼ cup chopped fresh cilantro

Lemon wedges

(RECIPE CONTINUES)

**Make the crab cakes:** In a large nonstick pan over medium-high heat, heat the oil. Add the corn, onion, and red pepper and cook until just tender, 5 minutes. Transfer the mixture to a food processor and pulse to form a coarse puree.

In a large bowl, add the corn mixture, shredded hearts of palm, breadcrumbs, mayonnaise, nori, parsley, Old Bay, mustard powder, salt, and pepper. Stir gently to combine.

On a large plate, place a generous layer of breadcrumbs. Line another plate or baking sheet with parchment. Using a ¼-cup measure, scoop out portions of the crab cake mixture, flatten slightly with your hands, and dredge in the breadcrumbs. Place on the parchment-lined plate and repeat with the remaining mixture.

In a large, deep nonstick or cast-iron pan over medium-high heat, add a thin layer of oil. When the oil is shimmering, working in batches if needed, fry the crab cakes until golden, about 2 minutes per side. Transfer to a plate and repeat with the remaining crab cakes.

**Serve:** Top each crab cake with a tablespoon or two of the mayo and sprinkle the cilantro on top. Serve with the lemon wedges.

# GORDITAS

There's not much more to this popular street food than fried masa stuffed to bursting with all kinds of different fillings until it basically resembles a fat pita pocket. (*Gordita* means "chubby.") We go supreme with black beans, vegan chorizo, salsa verde, avocado, cashew cream, and almond cotija. And to make sure all our savory bases are covered, we finish it off with some crispy rice paper chicharrones.

SERVES 6

### FOR THE CORN MASA

2 cups masa harina (such as Maseca)

1 teaspoon Himalayan salt

1⅓ cups warm water

### TO ASSEMBLE

Canola, rice bran, or other neutral oil, for frying

1 cup Black Beans (page 221)

1 cup vegan chorizo, crumbled if needed

½ cup Salsa Verde (page 191)

1 avocado, sliced

¼ cup Cashew Crema (page 184)

½ cup Almond Cotija (page 183)

½ cup chopped fresh cilantro

1 cup Rice Paper Chicharrones pieces (page 218)

**Make the corn masa:** In a large bowl, whisk together the masa harina and salt. Slowly add the warm water and mix until mostly combined. Use your hands to gently knead and press the mixture into one large ball of dough.

Turn the dough out onto a clean surface and divide into 6 equal pieces. Roll each piece into a ball and flatten one side just slightly. (This will serve

(RECIPE CONTINUES)

as the base of the gordita.) Set the dough balls on a plate and cover with a kitchen towel to keep them from drying out.

**Assemble:** In a Dutch oven, heavy-bottomed pot, or high-sided frying pan over medium-high heat, heat about 3 inches of oil to 375°F. Line a plate or baking sheet with a few layers of paper towels and place nearby for draining.

Working in batches if needed, fry the dough balls, turning frequently, until the dough is deep golden brown, 4 to 5 minutes. Using tongs, transfer the balls to the plate and let cool briefly. Cut through the center of each ball and open it up like a hamburger bun. Scoop out any excess raw dough and discard. Refry the hollowed halves for 1 to 2 minutes and transfer to the plate again to drain and cool completely.

Spread the black beans and chorizo on 6 of the halves. Top with the salsa verde and avocado slices and a drizzle of the cashew crema. Sprinkle the almond cotija and cilantro on top and finish with 1 or 2 pieces of the rice chicharrón. Serve with the other halves set alongside.

# MEXICAN-STYLE STREET CORN

It's easy to see why this is one of the most popular street foods in Mexico: It's a whole ear of corn schmeared with mayo (or spicy mayo, in this case), liberally sprinkled with cheese (or pumpkin seed parmesan), and brightened with fresh cilantro and lime. Lucky for you, it's also incredibly simple to re-create at home.

SERVES 8

4 ears fresh sweet corn, husked, silk removed, cut in half

1 teaspoon Himalayan salt

½ cup Spicy Mayo (page 177)

1 recipe Pumpkin Seed Parmesan (page 182)

¼ cup chopped fresh cilantro

Lime or lemon wedges, for serving

In a medium pot over medium-high heat, add the corn, salt, and enough water to cover. Bring to a boil and reduce the heat to medium. Cook the corn until just barely tender, 5 to 7 minutes. Using tongs, transfer the corn to a clean kitchen towel to dry and cool slightly. (Alternatively, you could grill the corn on a gas-fired grill or barbecue, turning frequently until lightly charred on all sides.)

Coat the corn with the spicy mayo, followed by the pumpkin seed parmesan. Place on a serving plate, garnish with the cilantro, and serve with lime wedges.

MEXICAN-STYLE STREET CORN

# GUACAMOLE CON TORTILLAS

Our version of this Mexican-restaurant staple goes back to its roots, more closely resembling what you'd get if you were strolling through a farmers market in Mexico City, where avocado vendors tend giant molcajetes full of ready-to-eat guac. We serve it alongside our homemade tortillas—the preferred vehicle for this condiment in Mexico—rather than fried tortilla chips (though you could sub those in, too, and no one would complain).

SERVES 4

### FOR THE GUACAMOLE

3 avocados, cut into 1-inch cubes

3 tablespoons chopped fresh cilantro, plus more for serving

1½ tablespoons fresh lemon juice

1½ tablespoons finely chopped red onion

1 teaspoon seeded and finely chopped jalapeño

½ teaspoon Himalayan salt

### FOR SERVING

8 Tortillas (page 209), or store-bought corn tortillas, warmed

Lime or lemon wedges

**Make the guacamole:** In a medium bowl, add the avocados, cilantro, lemon juice, red onion, jalapeño, and salt. Gently mash the mixture with a potato masher, aiming for a chunky texture.

**Serve:** Spread the guacamole on the tortillas and garnish with cilantro. Roll up and serve with lime wedges.

# NACHOS AL PASTOR

Chips and nacho cheese may not be true-blue Mexican food, but far be it from us to deprive you of this "Mexican" American favorite—Madre-style. We load up fresh tortilla chips with plenty of cashew nacho cheese plus our signature mushroom pastor that we pair with our pineapple habanero salsa (pastor and pineapple are a traditional team). Add some beans, salsa, and guac, and you've got a party on a plate.

SERVES 4

4 cups Tortilla Chips (page 15), or store-bought

1 cup Black Beans (page 221)

¼ cup Cashew Nacho Cheese (page 181)

⅓ cup Pineapple Habanero Salsa (page 15)

1 cup Mushroom Pastor (page 213)

¼ cup Pico de Gallo (page 194)

1 cup Guacamole (page 41)

On a large serving platter, spread out the tortilla chips in an even layer. Spoon the black beans over the chips, then layer the nacho cheese, pineapple salsa, mushroom pastor, and pico de gallo. Serve with the guacamole.

# REPOLLITOS FRITOS

This simple—and very popular—starter of crispy Brussels sprouts tossed in a fresh cilantro almond pesto is just about everyone's favorite way to indulge in more vegetables. Because the Brussels are blanched first, just kissed by the hot oil, and then topped with a fresh pesto, they don't feel heavy. The almonds will need to soak overnight, so plan accordingly when preparing this dish.

SERVES 4

## FOR THE CILANTRO ALMOND PESTO

½ cup almonds

1 cup packed fresh cilantro

3 tablespoons fresh lemon juice

1 tablespoon chopped garlic

½ small jalapeño, seeded and chopped

½ teaspoon Himalayan salt

⅓ cup extra-virgin olive oil

## FOR THE BRUSSELS SPROUTS

Himalayan salt, to taste

4 cups Brussels sprouts, trimmed and halved

Canola, rice bran, or other neutral oil, for frying

1 lemon, cut into wedges

**Make the pesto:** In a large jar or covered bowl, add the almonds and enough water to cover. Soak overnight, drain, and rinse.

In a food processor, add the almonds, cilantro, lemon juice, garlic, jalapeño, and salt. Pulse until well blended but not quite pureed. With the processor running, add the olive oil and process until combined.

(RECIPE CONTINUES)

**Make the Brussels sprouts:** Fill a large pot with salted water and bring to a boil over medium-high heat. While the water heats, prepare an ice bath in a large bowl nearby. Add the Brussels sprouts to the water and blanch until just tender, about 3 minutes. Using a skimmer or slotted spoon, remove the Brussels sprouts and place immediately in the ice bath. Let sit for 3 minutes and drain.

Spread a clean kitchen towel or a few layers of paper towels across a board or counter. Spread out the blanched Brussels sprouts on the towel and pat to dry as much as possible. (Removing most of the water now means less oil will sputter up while frying.)

In a Dutch oven, heavy-bottomed pot, or high-sided frying pan over high heat, heat about 3 inches of canola oil to 350°F. While the oil heats, line a baking sheet with paper towels for draining and place it nearby. Working in batches so as not to crowd the pot, fry the Brussels sprouts until lightly crispy, for about 3 minutes, flipping occasionally to fry evenly. Using a skimmer or slotted spoon, remove the fried Brussels sprouts and place on the baking sheet. Season immediately with salt. Repeat to fry the remaining Brussels sprouts.

In a large bowl, toss the Brussels sprouts with the cilantro almond pesto. Transfer to a plate and serve with the lemon wedges.

# MANGO SOPES

Sopes are a common midday offering from street-food carts, and they're the perfect handheld food for a quick bite or light lunch. They showcase a variety of toppings—beans, cheese, escabeche, salsa—that sit on top a round of masa slightly thicker than a tortilla. We offer a slightly updated sweet-savory version with mango salsa, but you could also change things up by using our Black Beans (page 221) or Madre Coconut Ceviche (page 27).

MAKES 10 SOPES

1 recipe Corn Masa (page 32)

Canola, rice bran, or other neutral oil, for frying

¾ cup Guacamole (page 41)

1 cup Quick-Pickled Cabbage (page 131)

½ cup Pico de Gallo (page 194)

½ cup Mango Salsa (page 15)

⅓ cup Cashew Crema (page 184)

¼ cup chopped fresh cilantro

Divide the corn masa into 10 equal pieces and roll each one into a ball. Cover the balls with a kitchen towel to keep them from drying out.

Place each ball between a folded sheet of plastic wrap and gently flatten into a 2-inch disk. Set each disk back under the kitchen towel to stay moist while you flatten the remaining balls.

In a heavy-bottomed, high-sided frying pan over medium-high heat, heat about 2 inches of oil to 375°F. Line a plate or baking sheet with a few layers of paper towels and place nearby for draining.

(RECIPE CONTINUES)

Working in batches, fry the disks for 30 seconds per side and transfer to the plate to cool slightly. Place a small water glass upside down over a kitchen towel. Place the disk on the base of the glass and press the edges down slightly so the disk forms a little round boat shape. Fry the sopes once more, flipping occasionally, until deeply golden brown, about 3 minutes, and transfer to the plate again to drain.

Fill each sope with a scoop of guacamole, followed by the quick-pickled cabbage, pico de gallo, and mango salsa. Drizzle the cashew crema on top and finish with the cilantro.

# EMPANADAS

These pocket-size bites are one of the original fusion foods of Mexico. When the British started mining for precious metals in Mexico, they brought with them stuffed pasties. Over time, people started making versions that could be parceled up as the perfect portable meal, oftentimes with plant-forward fillings like potatoes. What's remained is a delicious stuffed-and-fried snack, which we offer three ways: with jackfruit mixiote, pumpkin, and chorizo and potato.

## EMPANADA PASTRY

MAKES 12 EMPANADAS

1¾ cups cold coconut oil

4 cups all-purpose flour

1 tablespoon sugar

2 teaspoons baking powder

1½ teaspoons Himalayan salt

1 cup ice water

1 tablespoon plus 1 teaspoon apple cider vinegar

Using the shredder attachment on a food processor, shred the coconut oil. Transfer the shredded oil to a bowl, cover, and refrigerate.

Over a large bowl, sift together the flour, sugar, baking powder, and salt.

Place the bowl in the freezer for 15 minutes.

In a food processor, add the flour mixture and coconut oil and pulse until just combined. With the processor running, add the ice water and vinegar until a loose dough forms. Turn the dough out onto a clean surface and use your hands to press the dough into a ball. Divide the dough into 12 equal pieces (about 3 ounces each) and roll each one into a ball. Use a tortilla press or rolling pin to flatten the balls into roughly 6-inch circles. Place the dough circles between layers of parchment or plastic wrap and chill until ready to use.

(RECIPE CONTINUES)

# PUMPKIN

MAKES 12 EMPANADAS

## FOR THE PUMPKIN FILLING

1 tablespoon extra-virgin olive oil

1 medium onion, thinly sliced

1 cup thinly sliced cremini mushrooms

1½ cups diced pumpkin or butternut squash

1 teaspoon Himalayan salt

1 cup chopped kale

2 tablespoons chopped fresh mint

## FOR THE EMPANADAS

Canola, rice bran, or other neutral oil, for frying

1 recipe Empanada Pastry

1 cup Mole Negro (page 200)

½ cup Cashew Crema (page 184)

¼ cup pumpkin seeds, toasted until fragrant

¼ cup chopped fresh cilantro

**MAKE THE FILLING:** In a large nonstick or cast-iron pan over medium-high heat, heat the olive oil. Add the onions and mushrooms and cook, stirring, until the onions are translucent and the mushrooms have given off some moisture, about 8 minutes. Reduce the heat to medium and add the pumpkin and ½ teaspoon of the salt. Cook, stirring occasionally, until the squash is soft but holds its shape, about 10 minutes. Add the kale and the remaining ½ teaspoon salt and cook until the kale is just wilted, 3 minutes. Add the mint and stir to combine.

**MAKE THE EMPANADAS:** Place a few tablespoons of the pumpkin filling on one side of each pastry. Use your finger or a brush to moisten the edges of the pastry with water. Fold the pastry snugly over the filling, easing out any excess air, and press the edges together. Seal the edges with the tines of a fork or pinch together with your fingers. Transfer the assembled empanadas to a baking sheet or plate and cover with a kitchen towel to keep them from drying out.

In a Dutch oven, heavy-bottomed pot, or high-sided frying pan over medium-high heat, heat about 3 inches of oil to 350°F. Line a plate or baking sheet with a few layers of paper towels and place nearby for draining.

Working in batches, fry the empanadas until deep golden brown, 2 or 3 minutes per side. Transfer to the plate to drain and cool.

Top the empanadas with the mole negro and cashew crema and garnish with the pumpkin seeds and cilantro.

# JACKFRUIT MIXIOTE

MAKES 12 EMPANADAS

Canola, rice bran, or other neutral oil, for frying

1 recipe Jackfruit Mixiote (page 211)

1 recipe Empanada Pastry

1 cup Avocado Salsa Verde (page 105)

Place a few tablespoons of the jackfruit on one side of each pastry. Use your finger or a pastry brush to moisten the edges of the pastry with water. Fold the pastry snugly over the filling, easing out any excess air, and press the pastry edges together. Seal the edges with the tines of a fork or pinch together with your fingers. Transfer the assembled empanadas to a baking sheet or plate and cover with a kitchen towel to keep them from drying out.

In a Dutch oven, heavy-bottomed pot, or high-sided frying pan over medium-high heat, heat about 3 inches of oil to 350°F. Line a plate or baking sheet with a few layers of paper towels and place nearby for draining.

Working in batches, fry the empanadas until deep golden brown, 2 or 3 minutes per side. Transfer to the plate to drain and cool.

Serve with the avocado salsa verde for dipping.

# CHORIZO AND POTATO

MAKES 12 EMPANADAS

## FOR THE CHORIZO AND POTATO FILLING

2 medium potatoes, peeled and diced (about 1½ cups)

2 teaspoons extra-virgin olive oil

2 garlic cloves, chopped

½ cup vegan chorizo, crumbled if needed

¼ cup minced poblano pepper (stemmed and seeded)

Himalayan salt, to taste

(RECIPE CONTINUES)

## FOR THE EMPANADAS

Canola, rice bran, or other neutral oil, for frying

1 recipe Empanada Pastry

1 cup Avocado Salsa Verde (page 105)

MAKE THE FILLING: In a medium pot, add the potatoes and enough water to cover. Set over medium-high heat and bring to a boil. Reduce the heat to medium and boil the potatoes until fully cooked, about 8 minutes. Drain the potatoes.

In a large nonstick pan over medium-high heat, heat the olive oil. Add the garlic and cook for 1 minute, until very fragrant. Add the chorizo and poblanos and cook until the poblanos soften slightly, about 3 minutes. Add the potatoes and cook for another 5 minutes. Remove from the heat and add salt to taste.

MAKE THE EMPANADAS: Place a few tablespoons of the chorizo filling on one side of each pastry. Use your finger or a pastry brush to moisten the edges of the pastry with water. Fold the pastry snugly over the filling, easing out any excess air, and press the pastry edges together. Seal the edges with the tines of a fork or pinch together with your fingers. Transfer the assembled empanadas to a baking sheet or plate and cover with a kitchen towel to keep them from drying out.

In a Dutch oven, heavy-bottomed pot, or high-sided frying pan over medium-high heat, heat about 3 inches of oil to 350°F. Line a plate or baking sheet with a few layers of paper towels and place nearby for draining.

Working in batches, fry the empanadas until deep golden brown, 2 or 3 minutes per side. Transfer to the plate to drain and cool.

Serve with the avocado salsa verde for dipping.

# CHAPTER 2

# SOPAS & SALADS

# HEIRLOOM TOMATO SALAD

Many people don't realize it, but the north of Mexico—especially Baja California—is at the same latitude as the Mediterranean. As a result, amazing olive oil is produced there, and agricultural production is strong, featuring heirloom tomatoes, Mexican squash—which is similar to what we consider summer squash here in the States—and greens such as spinach, lettuces, arugula, and kale. This deceivingly simple salad showcases that bounty and brings it all together with a sweet-smoky dressing made from charred tortillas and piloncillo, or Mexican raw sugar.

SERVES 4

## FOR THE TORTILLA ASH DRESSING

10 Tortillas (page 209), or store-bought corn tortillas

¼ cup fresh lemon juice

¼ cup apple cider vinegar

1 ounce piloncillo, or 2 tablespoons packed dark brown sugar

1¼ cups extra-virgin olive oil

## FOR THE SALAD

2 Mexican squashes or zucchini, quartered

2 cups arugula

2 cups shredded romaine

2 cups shredded kale

1½ cups watercress

5 medium to large heirloom tomatoes, cut into wedges

½ cup chopped pecans

Edible flowers, for garnish (optional)

**Make the dressing:** Heat a grill pan or outdoor grill to medium-high heat. Using tongs, carefully char the tortillas until they're mostly blackened.

(RECIPE CONTINUES)

In a high-speed blender, add the blackened tortillas, lemon juice, vinegar, and piloncillo and blend until smooth. With the blender running, stream in the oil until it is fully incorporated.

**Make the salad:** Heat a grill pan or outdoor grill to medium-high heat. Grill the squash pieces until slightly charred, 3 to 5 minutes per side.

In a large bowl, add the arugula, romaine, kale, and watercress. Dress with a few spoonfuls of the dressing and toss to coat.

Transfer the dressed greens to a large serving platter. Place the tomatoes and grilled squash in and around the greens and garnish with the pecans and flowers, if using. Drizzle additional dressing on top. Store leftover dressing in a sealed jar in the refrigerator for up to 1 week.

# MADRE'S CHOPPED SALAD

For one of our most popular lunchtime offerings, we wanted to both give people a plant-based version of an unmistakable American classic and feature quintessentially Mexican ingredients like plenty of fresh avocado, chickpeas, and a cumin-tahini dressing.

SERVES 4

## FOR THE CUMIN-TAHINI DRESSING

¼ cup tahini

3 tablespoons fresh lemon juice

2 tablespoons extra-virgin olive oil

½ teaspoon ground cumin

¼ teaspoon cayenne

Himalayan salt and freshly cracked black pepper, to taste

## FOR THE SALAD

1 small Mexican squash or zucchini, sliced lengthwise into ½-inch planks

1 teaspoon extra-virgin olive oil

Himalayan salt and freshly ground black pepper, to taste

1 large head romaine, shredded

1 cup cooked chickpeas, drained and rinsed

1 cup cherry tomatoes, halved

¼ cup packed fresh basil leaves, chopped

6 sprigs fresh mint, leaves chopped

1 avocado, cubed

1 tablespoon sesame seeds

**Make the dressing:** In a medium bowl, whisk together the tahini, lemon juice, oil, cumin, cayenne, salt, and pepper until smooth. Taste and adjust the seasoning.

(RECIPE CONTINUES)

**Make the salad:** Heat a grill pan over medium-high heat. Brush the Mexican squash with the oil and season with the salt and pepper. Grill the Mexican squash until tender and beginning to soften, flipping occasionally to char lightly, 3 to 4 minutes per side. Remove to a cutting board and chop into bite-size pieces.

In a large bowl, add the romaine, chickpeas, tomatoes, basil, mint, and the grilled squash pieces. Add the dressing and toss to coat. Taste and adjust the seasoning, add the avocado and sesame seeds, and toss gently once more.

# ENSALADA DE VERANO

This "salad of summer" is inspired by the country markets of Mexico City, where you can always find fresh, simple salads showcasing the season's produce and not much more. Standouts among them are the cucumber and lettuce salads, which are typically drizzled with a barely there vinaigrette in order to let the veggies' natural flavor come through. This is our homage to the singular magic of quality, seasonal produce served as simply as nature intended.

SERVES 4

## FOR THE LEMON-THYME DRESSING

½ cup extra-virgin olive oil

Zest of ½ lemon plus ¼ cup fresh lemon juice

2 tablespoons honey

2 tablespoons apple cider vinegar

1½ teaspoons chopped fresh thyme leaves

1 small garlic clove, minced or grated on a Microplane

½ teaspoon Himalayan salt

## FOR THE SALAD

1 teaspoon extra-virgin olive oil

1 cup corn, fresh or frozen and thawed

6 cups baby arugula

2 Persian cucumbers, sliced in ½-inch rounds

1 cup cherry tomatoes, halved

1 avocado, cubed

½ red bell pepper, seeded and thinly sliced

¼ cup seeded and finely diced poblano pepper

¼ cup finely diced red onion

Himalayan salt, to taste

**Make the dressing:** In a medium bowl, add the oil, lemon zest, lemon juice, honey, vinegar, thyme, garlic, and salt and whisk thoroughly to combine.

**Make the salad:** In a large nonstick or cast-iron pan over medium-high heat, heat the oil. Add the corn and cook, stirring occasionally, until it has taken on a bit of color and char, about 8 minutes. Remove from the heat and let cool.

In a large bowl, add the arugula, cucumber, tomatoes, avocado, red pepper, poblano pepper, red onion, salt to taste, and the corn. Add the dressing and toss to coat. Taste and adjust the seasoning.

WATERMELON TIRADITO

# WATERMELON TIRADITO

When you're in places like Baja, Nayarit, and other states in the north where regional food is all about fresh fish and really great olive oil, if you say to the fish vendor, "Make me a tiradito," they'll take thin slices of fish and toss them on a plate (*tiradito* means "throw") with olive oil, salt, and fresh chile. It's about as light and fresh as it gets. For our version, we dehydrate watermelon to emulate that pink, fleshy sweetness you get from fish, then toss it with an herbaceous vinaigrette that showcases hoja santa, an herb that's native to Mexico and tastes like a hybrid of licorice, sassafras, mint, and tarragon. (Some people call it root beer plant.) There's also a guacachile, a green-heat salsa made with not much more than olive oil and jalapeños.

SERVES 4

1 seedless mini watermelon, rind removed, cut into ½-inch rounds

### FOR THE GUACACHILE

1 cup extra-virgin olive oil

8 jalapeños, stemmed, halved, and seeded

1 medium onion, cut into quarters

1 garlic clove

1½ teaspoons Himalayan salt

### FOR THE HOJA SANTA VINAIGRETTE

3 fresh hoja santa leaves (or 2 if using dried)

¼ cup fresh lemon juice

3 tablespoons agave nectar

¼ teaspoon Himalayan salt

¾ cup extra-virgin olive oil

### FOR SERVING

1 cup Tortilla Chips (page 15), or store-bought, broken into bite-size pieces

2 tomatillos, husks removed,
 diced

½ cup fresh cilantro leaves

½ cup fresh mint leaves, torn in
 half if large

2 tablespoons fresh lemon juice

1 tablespoon extra-virgin olive oil

Himalayan salt, to taste

¼ cup Coconut Bacon
 (page 223)

Preheat the oven to 200°F. Line two baking sheets with parchment.

Place the watermelon rounds on the parchment and bake for 6 hours, until the watermelon is dry yet still firm. Let cool completely.

**Make the guacachile:** In a medium saucepan over medium-high heat, add the oil, jalapeños, onion, garlic, and salt. Bring to a boil, reduce the heat to low, and simmer until the jalapeños are soft and have collapsed slightly, 20 to 25 minutes. Using an immersion blender, blend until smooth.

**Make the vinaigrette:** In a high-speed blender, add the hoja santa leaves, lemon juice, agave, and salt and blend until the leaves have broken down. With the blender running, slowly add the oil until the dressing is emulsified.

**Serve:** Cut the watermelon rounds into 2 × 4-inch pieces and shingle them on a large serving plate. In a medium bowl, add the tortilla chips, tomatillos, cilantro, mint, lemon juice, and oil. Toss to coat and season to taste with salt. Heap the salad on top of the watermelon and garnish with the coconut bacon. Drizzle the vinaigrette over the plate and dot with the guacachile. Serve with the remaining vinaigrette and guacachile on the side.

# TORTILLA SOUP

While you can find this rustic, comforting soup on menus in restaurants in Mexico, it's a dish that's mainly served up in people's own homes. We wanted it to feel every bit as loving, so we've stuck with tradition: a soul-warming broth of tomatoes and chiles plus standard-issue toppings like avocado, tortilla chips, and two kinds of "cheese" (cashew crema and pumpkin seed parmesan). To make this an even heartier meal, serve the soup alongside a bowl of Black Beans (page 221).

SERVES 6

### FOR THE SOUP

4 Roma or plum tomatoes

6 dried guajillo chiles, stemmed
    and seeded

6 cups vegetable broth

6 poblano peppers

6 cups thinly sliced cremini
    mushrooms

2 teaspoons Himalayan salt

### FOR SERVING

2 cups Tortilla Chips (page 15),
    or store-bought

½ cup Cashew Crema (page 184)

2 tablespoons Pumpkin Seed
    Parmesan (page 182)

1 avocado, cubed

**Make the soup:** Place the tomatoes in a large, dry cast-iron or nonstick pan. Place the pan over medium heat and allow the tomatoes to char and blister on all sides, turning occasionally, 15 to 20 minutes. In the final few minutes, add the guajillos and toast briefly, about 2 minutes. Transfer the tomatoes, guajillos, and 1 cup of the vegetable broth to a high-speed blender and blend until smooth.

(RECIPE CONTINUES)

In a large pot over medium-high heat, add the tomato mixture and the remaining 5 cups vegetable broth. Bring to a boil, reduce the heat to low, and simmer, covered, for 20 minutes.

Over a gas stove burner, roast the poblanos directly over a medium flame until completely blackened, about 5 minutes per side. (You can also do this on a charcoal grill or under a broiler.) Transfer the blackened peppers to a large bowl and cover tightly with plastic. Set aside to steam for 10 minutes.

Using your hands, remove the charred skin from the poblanos. Use your hands or a small knife to remove the stem and the seeds. Slice the peppers into thin, 2-inch strips.

Add the sliced poblanos, mushrooms, and salt to the soup and continue simmering for 5 minutes.

**Serve:** Ladle the soup into bowls and finish with the tortilla chips, crema, parmesan, and avocado.

# POZOLE

This is a dish that's meant to be made with love. It's usually reserved for celebrations and holidays, and because it's typically the same recipe that your mother or grandmother has been making for years, it truly feels like you're eating something special. There are three different types of pozole, depending on the chiles you use—red, green, and white—and we opt for red, mixing ancho chiles into a hearty, hominy- and chickpea-studded broth. And as is tradition, make sure you're never serving this without plenty of avocado, cabbage, and crema on the table.

SERVES 6

## FOR THE SOUP

4 dried ancho chiles, stemmed
　　and seeded

¼ cup extra-virgin olive oil

2 cups chopped onion

6 cups vegetable broth or water

3 garlic cloves, chopped

1 tablespoon apple cider vinegar

2 teaspoons ground cumin

1 teaspoon dried oregano

1 teaspoon agave nectar

1 whole clove

1 (29-ounce) can white hominy,
　　drained and rinsed

1 (15-ounce) can chickpeas,
　　drained and rinsed

½ teaspoon Himalayan salt, plus
　　more to taste

Freshly ground black pepper,
　　to taste

## FOR SERVING

2 avocados, cubed

1 cup shredded green or red
　　cabbage

½ cup thinly sliced or julienned
　　radishes

¾ cup Cashew Crema
　　(page 184)

½ cup chopped fresh cilantro

Lime wedges

(RECIPE CONTINUES)

**Make the pozole:** Heat a dry cast-iron pan or other heavy sauté pan over medium heat. Add the chiles and toast until fragrant and darkened in color, about 5 minutes. Transfer the chiles to a bowl and cover with cold water. Soak until soft, 20 minutes.

In a heavy pot over medium heat, heat the oil. Add the onion and cook, stirring, until golden, about 15 minutes.

Drain the chiles and add them to the pitcher of a high-speed blender. Add 1 cup of the broth, the garlic, vinegar, cumin, oregano, agave, and clove and blend until smooth.

Add the blended mixture to the pot with the onions, along with the remaining 5 cups of broth, the hominy, chickpeas, salt, and pepper. Increase the heat to high and bring to a boil. Reduce the heat to low and simmer until the hominy is very tender, about 20 minutes.

**Serve:** Ladle the soup into bowls and top with the avocado, cabbage, and radish. Drizzle the crema on top and finish with the cilantro. Serve with the lime wedges.

# WATERMELON GAZPACHO

We add strawberries and watermelon to this simple chilled soup to heighten the natural sweetness of the tomatoes, which get balanced out with bell peppers, garlic, vinegar, and olive oil. It's the perfect light lunch on a warm day.

SERVES 6

4 cups seeded and roughly chopped tomatoes

3½ cups cubed seedless watermelon

2½ cups strawberries, hulled and halved

½ red bell pepper, stemmed, seeded, and roughly chopped

½ small onion, roughly chopped

1 garlic clove

1 slice stale sourdough or country bread, roughly torn

¼ cup fresh mint leaves (from about 2 sprigs)

2 tablespoons red wine vinegar

¼ cup extra-virgin olive oil

1½ cups ice

2 teaspoons Himalayan salt

1 teaspoon freshly ground black pepper

Tortilla Chips (page 15), or store-bought, for serving

In a high-speed blender, add the tomatoes, watermelon, strawberries, red pepper, onion, and garlic. Blend until smooth. Add the bread, mint, and vinegar and blend again until smooth. With the blender running, slowly add the oil until emulsified. Add the ice, salt, and pepper and blend until smooth.

Pour into bowls and serve immediately with the tortilla chips.

# CREMA DE ELOTE

Even though this rich, creamy corn soup wouldn't have been possible without Spain bringing butter, cream, and milk to Mexico, we now know that we don't need to rely on these ingredients to make an equally luxurious, silky offering thanks to nondairy alternatives.

SERVES 4

### FOR THE SOUP

1 tablespoon extra-virgin olive oil

1 medium onion, chopped

Himalayan salt, to taste

2 garlic cloves, chopped

2 cups corn, fresh or frozen and thawed

4 cups unsweetened almond milk

### FOR SERVING

½ cup Almond Cotija (page 183)

Truffle oil, for drizzling

4 Tostadas (page 3), roughly broken up, or store-bought tortilla chips

**Make the soup:** In a large, heavy pot over medium-high heat, heat the oil. Add the onion and a pinch of salt and cook until the onion is translucent, 5 minutes. Add the garlic and cook for 1 minute. Reduce the heat to medium-low, add the corn, and cook, stirring occasionally, until the corn is tender, 10 to 15 minutes.

Transfer to a high-speed blender and add the almond milk. Blend until the corn has completely broken down and the soup is very smooth, about 5 minutes. Return the soup to the pot, using a fine-mesh sieve if desired to eliminate any pieces. Warm on low heat and season to taste.

**Serve:** Ladle the soup into bowls and garnish with the almond cotija and a drizzle of truffle oil. Serve with the tostadas.

# CHAPTER 3

# TORTAS & BOWLS

# TORTAS

Tortas are, pretty simply, sandwiches. They're what you find in lunch-boxes and on afternoon food carts, and they're no-frills, homey, and most importantly, loaded up with layers of flavor. The most common torta you'll find anywhere in Mexico is the Milanesa, which we put a Madre twist on by using crispy breaded eggplant instead of thin cuts of meat. We also offer our spin on the popular chorizo version and al pastor, with plenty of beans, vegan cheese, and spicy mayo to make sure they're a finger-licking mess in all the right ways. And then there's the Pambazo, a quintessentially Mexican sandwich where the roll first gets dunked in guajillo salsa, generously filled with spicy (vegan) chorizo and potatoes, then griddled until crisp. We highly recommend washing down any of these with a few cold cervezas.

## TORTA AL PASTOR

SERVES 4

2 teaspoons extra-virgin olive oil

1 cup Mushroom Pastor (page 213)

8 slices bread or 4 bolillo or ciabatta rolls, toasted

¼ cup Spicy Mayo (page 177)

4 slices vegan cheese (cheddar or mozzarella works well)

4 slices pineapple

¾ cup Guacamole (page 41)

½ cup Pico de Gallo (page 194)

In a medium nonstick pan over medium heat, heat the oil. Add the mushrooms and cook for 5 minutes, until warmed through.

Spread 1 slice of the toasted bread with the spicy mayo. Top with the warmed mushrooms, followed by the cheese, pineapple, guacamole, pico de gallo, and the other slice of bread. Repeat for the remaining bread and fillings.

# TORTA DE MILANESA

SERVES 4

1 small butternut squash, peeled, halved, seeded, and cut into ¼-inch slices

3 tablespoons extra-virgin olive oil

2½ teaspoons Himalayan salt, plus more as needed

1 teaspoon freshly ground black pepper

1 teaspoon paprika

1 small eggplant, cut into ¼-inch slices

Canola, rice bran, or other neutral oil, for frying

¾ cup all-purpose flour

¾ cup cornmeal

1 tablespoon sugar

1 tablespoon baking powder

1 tablespoon egg replacer

1 cup beer or sparkling water, plus more if needed

2 cups panko breadcrumbs

1 medium onion, sliced

¼ cup balsamic vinegar

4 bolillo rolls or ciabatta, split and toasted

½ cup Black Beans (page 221), warmed

¼ cup Spicy Mayo (page 177)

1 cup baby spinach

Preheat the oven to 375°F. Line a baking sheet with parchment.

In a large bowl, add the squash slices, 2 tablespoons of the olive oil, 1½ teaspoons of the salt, the pepper, and paprika and toss to coat. Arrange the squash on the baking sheet in a single layer and roast until tender, about 15 minutes.

Spread the eggplant slices on a few layers of paper towels and sprinkle both sides with salt. Let the eggplant sit for 15 minutes and blot any excess liquid with paper towels.

In a heavy-bottomed, high-sided frying pan over medium-high heat, heat about 2 inches of canola oil to 350°F. Line a baking sheet with a few layers of paper towels and place nearby for draining.

In a large bowl, add the flour, cornmeal, sugar, baking powder, egg replacer, and ½ teaspoon of the salt and whisk to combine. Add the beer and whisk until

(RECIPE CONTINUES)

the mixture is smooth and thick, like pancake batter, adding a splash more beer if needed.

In a medium bowl, add the breadcrumbs. Using a fork, dip the eggplant slices in the batter and turn to coat completely. Lift out of the batter, shake gently to remove any excess, and coat in the breadcrumbs.

Working in batches, fry the eggplant until golden brown, about 2 minutes per side. Transfer to the baking sheet to drain and repeat with the remaining eggplant slices.

In a medium nonstick pan over medium-high heat, heat the remaining tablespoon of olive oil. Add the onions, vinegar, and the remaining ½ teaspoon salt and cook until the onions begin to soften, about 5 minutes. Reduce the heat to medium-low and continue cooking, stirring occasionally, until the onions are caramelized and sweet, about 10 more minutes.

Spread the bottoms of each roll with the black beans and the tops with the spicy mayo. Build each torta starting with a layer of spinach, followed by a few slices of the fried eggplant, a few slices of squash, and a layer of caramelized onions. Top with the other half of the roll and serve.

# CHORIZO TORTA

SERVES 4

4 bolillo or ciabatta rolls, split and
toasted

1 cup Black Beans (page 221), warmed

½ cup vegan chorizo, crumbled as
needed, warmed

1 cup Quick-Pickled Cabbage
(page 131)

1 cup Pico de Gallo (page 194)

1 avocado, sliced

½ cup Cashew Crema (page 184)

Spread the bottoms of each roll with
the beans, then the chorizo. Top with
a layer of the pickled cabbage and pico
de gallo. Place the sliced avocado on top
and drizzle with the crema. Top with the
other half of the roll and serve.

# PAMBAZOS

SERVES 4

6 dried guajillo chiles

1 cup roughly chopped onion (about ¼ onion)

3 garlic cloves

1 teaspoon Himalayan salt

½ teaspoon ground cumin

3 medium Yukon Gold potatoes, peeled

2 tablespoons extra-virgin olive oil, plus more if needed

1 cup vegan chorizo, crumbled as needed

4 bolillo or ciabatta rolls, split

½ cup Black Beans (page 221)

4 cups shredded romaine lettuce

½ cup Almond Cotija (page 183)

½ cup Cashew Crema (page 184)

1 cup Salsa Roja (page 190)

In a high-speed blender, add the chiles, onion, garlic, salt, cumin, and 2 tablespoons of water and blend until smooth. Add more water, a teaspoon or two at a time, if needed to loosen the sauce.

In a medium saucepan over medium-high heat, add the potatoes and enough water to cover. Bring to a boil and cook until tender, 10 to 15 minutes. Drain and cut the potatoes into ½-inch cubes.

In a large nonstick pan over medium-high heat, heat 1 tablespoon of the oil. Reduce the heat to medium and add the chorizo. Cook until the oil has taken on color from the chorizo, about 3 minutes. Add the cubed potatoes and cook, stirring occasionally, for 10 minutes. Remove the pan from the heat and set aside.

Pour the guajillo sauce into a wide, shallow bowl. Dip the open halves of each roll in the sauce briefly—just long enough to moisten the bread but not long enough for it to soak all the way through. Spread 2 tablespoons of the black beans on each roll and fill with about a cup of the chorizo mixture.

In a large nonstick pan over medium-high heat, heat the remaining tablespoon of oil. Fry each sandwich until the bread is crisp and just golden, about 2 minutes per side. Add more oil to the pan as you go, if needed.

Add a layer of the lettuce, the almond cotija, and a drizzle of the cashew crema inside each warmed sandwich. Serve with the salsa roja on the side.

# BLACK BEAN BURGERS

There's nothing sexier than a big, meaty (meat-free) burger, and this is no exception. We made a patty using our signature Madre black beans as the base, which give the burger the toothsome heartiness you're looking for. But we're not in the business of heavy, weigh-you-down meals, so we added a bright, spicy pineapple slaw to put a little pep in this burger's step.

SERVES 6

## FOR THE BURGERS

¼ cup extra-virgin olive oil

1½ cups shredded red beets

1½ cups sliced white mushrooms

1½ cups diced onion

1 garlic clove, minced

¼ teaspoon chipotle powder

¼ teaspoon ground cumin

1½ cups cooked brown rice

1½ cups Black Beans (page 221)

3 tablespoons ground pumpkin seeds

3 tablespoons rolled oats

½ teaspoon Himalayan salt

## FOR THE PINEAPPLE COLESLAW

4 cups shredded green cabbage

1⅓ cups Pineapple Habanero Salsa (page 15), liquid drained

½ cup chopped fresh cilantro

½ cup vegan mayonnaise

½ jalapeño, stemmed, seeded, and finely minced

Himalayan salt, to taste

## FOR ASSEMBLY

6 brioche buns, sliced, and toasted if desired

1 cup Escabeche (page 215), diced

2 avocados, sliced

3 cups shredded romaine lettuce

3 tomatoes, sliced

½ cup Spicy Mayo (page 177)

**Make the burgers:** In a large nonstick pan over medium-high heat, heat 1 tablespoon of the oil. Add the beets, mushrooms, onions, garlic, chipotle powder, and cumin and cook until the onion is translucent and the mushrooms and beets have lost some moisture, about 10 minutes.

Transfer the mixture to a large bowl and add the rice, beans, pumpkin seeds, oats, and salt. Using a wooden spoon or spatula, mix thoroughly to combine. Using your hands, divide the mixture into 6 equal patties.

In a large nonstick or cast-iron pan over medium-high heat, heat the remaining 3 tablespoons oil. Cook the patties until crisped and browned, 4 to 5 minutes per side.

**Make the coleslaw:** In a medium bowl, add the cabbage, salsa, cilantro, mayo, and jalapeño. Mix to combine and season with salt to taste.

**Assemble:** Place a burger patty on each bun and top with the escabeche, a few avocado slices, romaine, and a few slices of tomato. Spread the spicy mayo on the top bun. Serve with the pineapple coleslaw.

# BURRITO BOWL

You like burritos. You like salad. So we've given you both, with a lighter, brighter take on the original. It's definitely a nod toward the fresh, flavor-forward spirit of traditional Mexican food, but still scratches the itch when you want something that'll fill you up.

SERVES 4

2 heads romaine, shredded

2 cups Black Beans (page 221)

2½ cups cooked brown rice

½ cup crumbled vegan chorizo

1 cup Pico de Gallo (page 194)

1 cup Guacamole (page 41)

½ cup Cashew Crema (page 184)

¼ cup pumpkin seeds

¼ cup chopped fresh cilantro

Divide the shredded romaine among four bowls. Divide and add the black beans on one side of each bowl and the brown rice on the other. Top with the chorizo and a scoop of the pico de gallo and guacamole. Drizzle the cashew crema over the bowls and scatter the pumpkin seeds and cilantro on top.

# CHEF'S BOWL

You frequently see Mexican squash—which is similar to zucchini—in Mexican home cooking, so we wanted to take that same humble ingredient and make it the focal point of this bowl, along with loads of fresh greens. By adding mango salsa plus a vibrant green rice and a simple cumin-spiked sesame dressing, the whole plate gets elevated into so much more than your usual salad.

SERVES 4

2 tablespoons extra-virgin olive oil

2 garlic cloves, chopped

4 cups cauliflower florets, cut into bite-size pieces

2 cups chopped carrots

2 cups chopped Mexican squash or zucchini

Himalayan salt, to taste

¼ cup white wine

8 cups chopped kale

Green Rice (page 222)

1 cup Mango Salsa (page 15)

1 avocado, cubed

1 cup sunflower, broccoli, or other favorite sprouts, for garnish (optional)

½ cup capers, drained

1 cup Cumin-Tahini Dressing (page 61)

In a large nonstick sauté pan over medium-high heat, heat 1 tablespoon of the oil. Add half of the chopped garlic, the cauliflower, carrots, Mexican squash, and salt to taste and cook, stirring frequently, until the cauliflower is just tender, about 8 minutes. Deglaze the pan with the white wine and stir until the liquid has evaporated. Transfer the cooked vegetables to a plate.

(RECIPE CONTINUES)

Return the pan to medium-high heat and heat the remaining tablespoon of oil. Add the remaining garlic and the kale. Add salt to taste and cook, stirring frequently, until the kale has wilted and collapsed but is still a vibrant green, about 8 minutes.

To serve, divide the green rice among four bowls. Divide the cooked cauliflower mixture among the bowls, placing it along one side of the bowl. Repeat with the kale, placing it on the other side of the bowl. Top the bowls with the mango salsa and the avocado, and garnish with the sprouts (if using) and the capers. Drizzle the dressing on top.

# TROPICAL BOWL

This dish puts the *sol* in a bowl that calls to mind the Mexico coast with all its tropical fruits and coconut. We take a bed of coconut rice and cumin-spiced lentils and drizzle it with a peanut-coconut sauce plus a dose of pineapple habanero salsa. For how hearty and filling this dish is, it's delightfully fresh and bright.

SERVES 4

**FOR THE COCONUT RICE**

2 teaspoons coconut oil

1⅓ cups brown basmati rice

1 (13.5-ounce) can full-fat coconut milk

⅓ cup unsweetened coconut flakes

1 teaspoon Himalayan salt

**FOR THE FRENCH LENTILS**

1 tablespoon extra-virgin olive oil

½ cup diced onion

¼ cup diced carrot

¼ cup diced celery

1 garlic clove, minced

½ teaspoon ground cumin

1 cup dried French lentils, picked over and rinsed

1 bay leaf

1 teaspoon Himalayan salt

½ teaspoon freshly ground black pepper

**FOR THE PEANUT SAUCE**

1 cup unsweetened peanut butter

⅔ cup full-fat coconut milk

⅔ cup fresh cilantro leaves

⅓ cup fresh lime juice

1 tablespoon plus 1 teaspoon ginger juice

1 tablespoon plus 1 teaspoon agave nectar

2 teaspoons tamari soy sauce

2 teaspoons chopped jalapeño

1 small garlic clove

1 teaspoon Himalayan salt

**(INGREDIENTS AND RECIPE CONTINUE)**

## FOR ASSEMBLY

12 cups loosely packed fresh baby
  spinach

1 cup Pico de Gallo (page 194)

1 cup Pineapple Habanero Salsa
  (page 15)

1 avocado, cubed

¼ cup pumpkin seeds

¼ cup fresh cilantro leaves

**Make the coconut rice:** In a large saucepan over medium-high heat, heat the coconut oil. Add the rice and toast in the oil for a few minutes, until fragrant. Add the coconut milk, coconut flakes, salt, and 1 cup of water and bring to a boil. Reduce the heat to low, cover, and simmer undisturbed for 45 minutes. Leaving the pan covered, remove from the heat and rest for 15 minutes. Fluff with a fork, taste, and adjust the seasoning.

**Make the lentils:** In a medium saucepan over medium-high heat, heat the olive oil. Add the onion, carrot, celery, garlic, and cumin and cook, stirring, until the onion has softened and the mixture begins to caramelize, about 10 minutes. Add the lentils, bay leaf, salt, pepper, and 3 cups of water and bring to a boil. Reduce the heat to low, cover, and simmer until the lentils are tender, 20 to 25 minutes.

**Make the peanut sauce:** In a high-speed blender, add the peanut butter, coconut milk, cilantro, lime juice, ginger juice, agave, tamari, jalapeño, garlic, and salt. Blend until smooth.

**Assemble the bowls:** Divide the spinach among four bowls and add a large scoop of the French lentils and coconut rice. Top with the pico de gallo, pineapple salsa, and avocado. Dress with the peanut sauce and garnish with the pumpkin seeds and cilantro.

CHAPTER 4

MAINS

# CHORIZO PLANTAIN QUESADILLAS

In Chiapas and Oaxaca, plantains are oftentimes found in savory fillings with onions, garlic, tomato, and chiles. There's still a tiny bit of sweetness peeking through, but it's balanced by the aromatics, as well as by the avocado salsa verde that we serve with this very traditional version of a quesadilla (sans cheese). We highly recommend some pickles or Escabeche (page 215) alongside too.

SERVES 6

## FOR THE AVOCADO SALSA VERDE

1 avocado, cubed

1 cup Salsa Verde (page 191)

1 tablespoon extra-virgin olive oil

1 teaspoon Himalayan salt

## FOR THE QUESADILLAS

¼ cup extra-virgin olive oil

1 small onion, chopped

4 garlic cloves, chopped

2 Roma or plum tomatoes, diced

½ cup vegan chorizo, crumbled if needed

2 large, very ripe plantains (skin should be black or nearly black), diced

1 teaspoon Himalayan salt

1 teaspoon ground cumin

½ teaspoon chipotle powder

6 Tortillas (page 209), or store-bought corn tortillas, warmed

¾ cup Cashew Crema (page 184)

¼ cup chopped fresh cilantro

**Make the avocado salsa:** In a high-speed blender, add the avocado, salsa verde, oil, and salt and blend until smooth and creamy.

(RECIPE CONTINUES)

**Make the quesadillas:** In a large nonstick sauté pan over medium-high heat, heat 1 tablespoon of the oil. Add the onion and cook until soft and translucent, about 5 minutes. Reduce the heat to medium, add the garlic, and cook for another 2 minutes. Add the tomato and chorizo and cook until the tomatoes have cooked down, about 5 minutes.

Increase the heat to medium-high and add the remaining 3 tablespoons oil. Once the oil is hot, add the plantains. Cook, stirring occasionally, until the edges of the plantains begin to brown and crisp, about 10 minutes. Add the salt, cumin, and chipotle powder and cook for 5 more minutes to let the flavors come together.

Fill each tortilla with some of the chorizo plantain mixture and fold the tortilla over. Crisp the quesadilla in the skillet for 1 to 2 minutes per side. Top with the avocado salsa and cashew crema, and garnish with the cilantro.

# CALABAZA AND ONION QUESADILLAS

Calabaza squash is a foundational ingredient in Mexican heritage cooking, so what better way to show it off than embracing its sweet creaminess and sandwiching it with some cashew nacho cheese in tortillas for the ultimate sweet-savory combo.

SERVES 4

8 Tortillas (page 209), or store-bought corn tortillas, warmed

2 cups Pumpkin Filling (page 52)

3/4 cup Cashew Nacho Cheese (page 181)

Pumpkin Seed Salsa (page 195)

1 cup Cashew Crema (page 184)

1/4 cup pumpkin seeds, toasted until fragrant

1/4 cup chopped fresh cilantro

Heat a medium sauté pan over medium-high heat.

Fill each tortilla with about 1/4 cup of the pumpkin filling and a few tablespoons of the nacho cheese. Fold the tortilla over and crisp the quesadilla in the pan for 1 to 2 minutes per side.

Serve the quesadillas with the pumpkin seed salsa and cashew crema. Garnish with the pumpkin seeds and cilantro.

# CHILAQUILES

This dish has a reputation for being the ultimate hangover cure, and far be it from us to put a stop to that legacy. Traditionally it was made with old tortillas that were fried then simmered in salsa (and served to prisoners, where this dish has its humble roots), but now it's perfectly acceptable to toss in tortilla chips (especially stale ones, if you have some you have to use up). Top it off with black beans and crema, and you have a satisfying meal, regardless of whether you had one too many the night before.

SERVES 2

4 cups Tortilla Chips (page 15), or store-bought

2 cups Salsa Roja (page 190), warmed

1 tablespoon diced yellow onion

½ avocado, sliced

¼ cup Cashew Crema (page 184)

2 tablespoons chopped fresh cilantro

2 cups Black Beans (page 221), warmed

In a large bowl, add the chips and salsa roja and toss to coat the chips. Transfer the coated chips to a plate and top with the onion and avocado. Drizzle the crema on top and garnish with the cilantro. Serve with the black beans on the side.

CHILAQUILES

# CHIMICHANGAS

These might be more Tex-Mex than Mex-Mex, but they're a total crowd-pleaser, and we're not about to deprive the people of tortillas that have been stuffed with potatoes, chorizo, cashew nacho cheese, and a slow-cooked red pepper sauce; deep-fried; then smothered in salsa, guac, and cashew crema.

SERVES 4

## FOR THE RED PEPPER CONFIT

1 tablespoon extra-virgin olive oil

1 medium red bell pepper, sliced ½-inch thick

1 medium onion, thinly sliced

½ teaspoon Himalayan salt

½ teaspoon dried oregano

## FOR THE CHIMICHANGAS

2 medium potatoes, peeled and diced

1 teaspoon extra-virgin olive oil

¼ teaspoon Himalayan salt

4 large flour tortillas, warmed

1 cup vegan chorizo, crumbled if needed

1 cup Black Beans (page 221)

½ cup Cashew Nacho Cheese (page 181)

Canola, rice bran, or other neutral oil, for frying

## FOR SERVING

1 cup Salsa Roja (page 190)

1 cup Guacamole (page 41)

½ cup Cashew Crema (page 184)

¼ cup pumpkin seeds

**Make the confit:** In a large nonstick or cast-iron pan over medium-high heat, heat the olive oil. Add the peppers and onions and cook, stirring, until they begin to soften, 8 minutes. Add the salt and oregano, reduce the

(RECIPE CONTINUES)

heat to medium-low, and continue cooking until the mixture is very soft and sweet, about 25 more minutes.

**Make the chimichangas:** Preheat the oven to 400°F. Line a baking sheet with parchment.

In a medium bowl, add the potatoes, olive oil, and salt and toss to coat. Spread the potatoes out on the baking sheet and roast until the potatoes are cooked through and beginning to crisp along the edges, about 15 minutes.

Divide the potatoes evenly among the tortillas, placing them in the middle of each tortilla and leaving about 2 inches around the sides of the tortilla for rolling. Repeat with about ¼ cup each of the red pepper confit, the chorizo, and the black beans. Drizzle the nacho cheese on top.

Fold the sides of the tortilla over the fillings, then fold one of the ends over. Roll into a packet and, if needed, secure with skewers or toothpicks.

In a heavy-bottomed, high-sided frying pan over medium-high heat, heat about 2 inches of canola oil to 350°F. Line a plate or baking sheet with a few layers of paper towels and place nearby for draining.

Fry each chimichanga until deep golden brown, 3 to 4 minutes per side, then transfer to the plate to drain.

**Serve:** Top each chimichanga with a layer of salsa roja and a scoop of guacamole. Drizzle the cashew crema on top and finish with the pumpkin seeds.

# CHILES RELLENOS

These stuffed, mole-draped peppers are a re-creation of a homey classic, but instead of the cheese you typically find inside, we showcase huitlacoche. While it's technically a fungus that grows on corn, we like to think of huitlacoche as the Mexican truffle, imparting earthy, mushroomy flavor. You can typically find it in Mexican markets sold in cans or jars.

SERVES 4

4 poblano peppers

1 tablespoon extra-virgin olive oil

1 cup chopped onion

2 garlic cloves, chopped

2 cups diced Roma or plum tomatoes

½ cup chopped Mexican squash or zucchini

Himalayan salt, to taste

1 cup corn, fresh or frozen and thawed

1½ cups huitlacoche

2 cups Black Bean Mole (page 202)

½ cup chopped fresh cilantro

Green Rice (page 222), for serving (optional)

Crispy onions, for serving (optional)

Over a gas stove burner, roast the poblanos directly over a medium flame until completely blackened, about 5 minutes per side. (You can also do this on a charcoal grill or under a broiler.) Transfer the blackened peppers to a large bowl and cover tightly with plastic. Set aside to steam for 10 minutes.

In a large nonstick or cast-iron pan over medium-high heat, heat the oil. Add the onion and garlic and cook, stirring, until the onion begins to soften, about 5 minutes. Add the tomato, Mexican squash, and salt to

(RECIPE CONTINUES)

taste and cook until the squash is tender, about 5 more minutes. Add the corn and huitlacoche and cook until the corn is just tender, 5 minutes. Taste and adjust the seasoning.

Using your hands or a paper towel, remove all the charred skin from the poblanos, if desired. Use a small knife to open the poblanos lengthwise and scrape out the seeds and veins, leaving the stem intact. Spoon about ½ cup of the corn mixture into each poblano.

Ladle the mole over the top and sprinkle with the cilantro. Serve with green rice and crispy onions, if desired.

# TAMALES VERDES

While tamales have become a fixture on the dinner menu in most Mexican restaurants, in Mexico they're typically eaten in the morning for breakfast. You usually find them offered on the streets—especially by bicycle vendors—and they come stuffed with almost any filling imaginable. But the tamal verde is by far the queen of the tamales, and it's what we offer, using salsa verde–braised jackfruit. Forming these little masa hot pockets, tucking them into corn husks, and steaming them is a bit of a process, but the steps are simple and the results unparalleled.

SERVES 8 (MAKES ABOUT 16 TAMALES)

## FOR THE TAMALES

16 dried corn husks, plus more for lining the pot

1 cup vegetable shortening

1½ teaspoons Himalayan salt

1½ teaspoons baking powder

3 cups masa harina (such as Maseca)

1 cup vegetable broth, plus more as needed

## FOR THE FILLING

2 tablespoons extra-virgin olive oil

1½ cups chopped onion

1 cup jackfruit, drained and rinsed

2 garlic cloves, chopped

¾ cup Salsa Verde (page 191)

1 teaspoon Himalayan salt

1 cup fresh purslane or baby spinach

## FOR SERVING

1 cup Salsa Verde (page 191)

½ cup Cashew Crema (page 184)

2 cups Pico de Gallo (page 194), optional

(RECIPE CONTINUES)

**Make the tamales:** Place the corn husks in a large stockpot and cover with hot water. Place a small plate on top of the husks to keep them submerged. Let stand until the husks are pliable, about 2 hours.

In the bowl of a stand mixer fitted with the paddle attachment, add the shortening, salt, and baking powder. Beat on medium-high speed until the mixture is light and fluffy, about 1 minute. Reduce the speed to medium-low and, with the mixer running, add the masa harina in thirds, waiting to add more until the flour is incorporated. Slowly add the broth and continue mixing for about 1 more minute.

Fill a small glass with cold water, scoop out a half-teaspoon dollop of the dough, and place it in the water. If it floats and holds its shape, taste and add more salt if desired. If it sinks, mix the dough for another minute, test again, and repeat as needed.

Cover and chill the dough for 1 hour to let it rest. Let it come back to room temperature, adding a splash more water or vegetable broth if needed to resoften the dough.

**Make the filling:** In a large nonstick or cast-iron pan over medium-high heat, heat the oil. Add the onion and cook until it begins to soften, about 5 minutes. Add the jackfruit and garlic and continue cooking, stirring occasionally, until the jackfruit is soft and broken down, 10 to 12 more minutes. Add the salsa verde and the salt and simmer for 1 minute. Remove from the heat and add the purslane, folding and stirring to help it wilt.

**Assemble the tamales:** Lay out a corn husk with the tapered end facing you and wipe off any remaining water. Scoop about ¼ cup of the dough about a third of the way from the top of the husk and press it into about a 4-inch square. Spoon a few tablespoons of the filling down the center of the square. Using the sides of the husk, lift the sides of the dough up around the filling and press lightly to seal it. Fold the sides of the husk over each other into a tube shape, then fold the tapered end under, pressing down where the mixture ends inside and using the fold as another seal. Set aside on a baking sheet, folded side down, and repeat with the remaining tamales.

In a tall stockpot or soup pot, add a few inches of water. Place a rack or steamer basket in the bottom of the pot, making sure the water is below the level of the rack. Line the rack with a few corn husks—this protects the tamales from direct contact with the steam and adds flavor. Place the tamales vertically, open side up, inside the pot, leaving a bit of room between them so they can expand as they cook. Add another layer of corn husks on top and cover. Turn the heat to medium and let the tamales steam until the husks easily pull away from the tamales, about 45 minutes. Remove from the heat and let the tamales stand in the steamer for 15 minutes to firm up.

**Serve:** Spoon the salsa verde over the tamales and drizzle with the cashew crema. Serve with pico de gallo, if desired.

# UCHEPOS

This dish is thought to have originated in Michoacán, but you'll find it all over the Mexican republic under both its original name and "corn tamal." It's essentially a sweeter, softer cousin of Tamales Verdes (page 119), using fresh sweet corn instead of masa harina and butter (vegan, in our case) and milk (almond) to make the mixture softer and richer. Uchepos can be served on their own or, as here, accompanied by salsa verde, almond cotija cheese, or cashew crema.

MAKES 8 UCHEPOS

8 ears sweet corn, kernels removed and reserved, husks reserved

1 cup coconut sugar

3 tablespoons unsweetened almond milk

1 teaspoon Himalayan salt, plus more to taste

½ cup vegan butter

3 poblano peppers, stemmed, seeded, and thinly sliced

1 medium onion, thinly sliced

2 cups Salsa Verde (page 191)

1 cup Cashew Crema (page 184)

1 cup Almond Cotija (page 183)

½ cup chopped fresh cilantro

In a food processor, add the corn kernels and pulse into a chunky puree. Add the coconut sugar, almond milk, and salt and process until smooth.

Each uchepo will need at least two of the fresh corn husks to wrap it. Layer the husks a couple of inches apart, with the tapered end facing you. Scoop about ¼ cup of the dough about a third of the way from the top of the husk and press it into about a 4-inch square. Gently lift the sides of the husk up around the filling and press lightly to seal it. Fold the sides of the husk over each other into a tube shape, then fold the tapered end under, pressing

(RECIPE CONTINUES)

down where the mixture ends inside and using the fold as another seal. Set aside on a baking sheet, folded side down, and repeat with the remaining uchepos.

In a tall stockpot or soup pot, add a few inches of water. Place a rack or steamer basket in the bottom of the pot, making sure the water is below the level of the rack. Line the rack with a few corn husks. Place the uchepos vertically, open side up, inside the pot. Tuck in any extra husks between the uchepos to keep them from moving around too much as they cook. Add another layer of corn husks on top and cover. Turn the heat to medium and let the uchepos steam until the husks easily pull away from the filling, about 55 minutes. Remove from the heat and let the uchepos stand in the steamer for 5 minutes to firm up.

While the uchepos steam, make the sauce. In a large nonstick or cast-iron pan over medium-high heat, add ¼ cup of the butter. Add the poblanos, onion, and salt to taste and cook until the peppers have softened and the onions are translucent, about 10 minutes. Add the salsa verde and cook until the salsa is heated through and incorporated with the poblanos and onions, 5 to 10 minutes.

In a medium nonstick pan over medium heat, melt a tablespoon or two of the butter. Unwrap the steamed uchepos and brown each one in the butter for about 2 minutes per side. Transfer the browned uchepos to the salsa verde mixture and spoon some of the sauce over the uchepos. Repeat with the remaining uchepos, adding more butter to the pan if needed as you brown them.

Serve the uchepos bathed in the sauce or return each uchepo to a husk and serve individually. Garnish with a drizzle of the crema, the almond cotija, and cilantro.

# BLACK BEAN TETELAS

This is street food straight out of Oaxaca, where you frequently see these crispy triangular black bean–filled parcels that have been smothered in cream and salsa. There's no point in improving on perfection, so we honored the traditional black bean filling, but we couldn't resist adding our own twist of serving the masa pockets with a crema-like cauliflower puree.

SERVES 6

**FOR THE CAULIFLOWER PUREE**

4 cups cauliflower florets

2 tablespoons extra-virgin olive oil

4 garlic cloves, minced

Himalayan salt, to taste

2 cups shredded vegan cheddar cheese

2 tablespoons vegan butter

**FOR THE TETELAS**

½ recipe Corn Masa (page 32)

1 cup Black Beans (page 221)

1 tablespoon extra-virgin olive oil

1 cup Salsa Roja (page 190), optional

1 avocado, sliced

½ cup chopped fresh cilantro or microgreens

**Make the cauliflower puree:** Preheat the oven to 400°F. Line a baking sheet with parchment.

In a large bowl, add the cauliflower, oil, garlic, and a large pinch of salt. Toss to coat. Spread the cauliflower out on the baking sheet and roast until the cauliflower is tender, about 15 minutes.

In a high-speed blender, add the roasted cauliflower, cheese, and butter, and blend until smooth. Taste and adjust salt as needed.

(RECIPE CONTINUES)

**Make the tetelas:** Divide the corn masa into 6 small balls. Using a tortilla press or a rolling pin, flatten the dough into a thin tortilla.

Spread a few tablespoons of the black beans in the center of the tortilla. Fold the three sides inward to create a triangle shape, overlapping the edges to seal the tetela. Repeat with the remaining black beans and tortillas.

In a large nonstick pan over medium-high heat, heat 1 teaspoon of the oil. Cook each tetela until just crisp, 1 to 2 minutes per side. Repeat with the remaining tetelas, adding more oil, 1 teaspoon or so at a time, as needed.

Spread the cauliflower puree on six small plates. Arrange the tetelas on top and finish with the salsa roja (if using), avocado, and cilantro.

TACOS

# MADRE TACOS

We like to say that with this dish you have the whole spirit of a country in four letters. Tacos are pretty much the official food of Mexico—you can find them from the north to the south, each version showcasing a regional specialty or anything you want to throw in a tortilla (there are no rules when it comes to tacos). They're a snack, they're a meal (breakfast, lunch, or dinner), and they're a whole social concept in and of themselves. Pretty much everyone—Mexican or otherwise—is always on the hunt for the best tacos. So we rounded up the best of the best, put our plant-based spin on traditional techniques and flavors, then threw them in a basket for your handheld, mouth-stuffing, drip-down-your-chin indulgence.

The Madre tacos that we always have in rotation include:

Mixiote, jackfruit that has been slow cooked in a rich, spiced adobo sauce;

Beer-Battered Portobello, our nod to the classic Baja fish taco;

Albóndigas, black bean and beet "meatballs" that get fried and tossed with crispy onions and cashew crema;

Mushroom Pastor, including the classic pineapple sidekick and smoky black salsa;

Coconut, a playful, modern addition to an otherwise classic lineup that we make even more interesting with an addition of a Mexican kimchi.

# BEER-BATTERED PORTOBELLO MUSHROOM MADRE TACOS

MAKES 8 TACOS

## FOR THE QUICK-PICKLED CABBAGE

1 garlic clove, cut in half

2 cups thinly shredded green cabbage

1 tablespoon apple cider vinegar

½ teaspoon Himalayan salt

## FOR THE MUSHROOMS

Canola, rice bran, or other neutral oil, for frying

¾ cup all-purpose flour

¾ cup cornmeal

1 tablespoon sugar

1 tablespoon baking powder

1 tablespoon egg replacer

½ teaspoon Himalayan salt, plus more for sprinkling

1 cup beer or sparkling water, plus more if needed

2 cups panko breadcrumbs

2 portobello mushroom caps, stems removed, cut into 1-inch strips

## FOR SERVING

8 Tortillas (page 209), or store-bought corn tortillas, warmed

½ cup Spicy Mayo (page 177)

¼ cup Salsa Brava (page 193)

¼ cup chopped fresh cilantro

Lime wedges

MAKE THE CABBAGE: Rub the cut side of the garlic clove around the inside of a large bowl. Discard the garlic or save for another use. In the bowl, add the cabbage, vinegar, and salt and toss to combine. Let sit while you make the mushrooms.

MAKE THE MUSHROOMS: In a heavy-bottomed, high-sided frying pan over medium-high heat, heat about 2 inches of oil to 350°F. Line a plate or baking sheet with a few layers of paper towels and place nearby for draining.

In a large bowl, add the flour, cornmeal, sugar, baking powder, egg replacer, and salt and whisk to combine. Add the beer

(RECIPE CONTINUES)

and whisk until the mixture is smooth and thick, like pancake batter, adding a splash more beer if needed.

In a medium bowl, add the breadcrumbs. Using a fork, dip the mushrooms in the batter and turn to coat completely. Lift out of the batter, shake gently to remove any excess, and roll the mushrooms in the breadcrumbs.

Working in batches so as not to crowd the pan, fry the mushroom strips in the hot oil until golden brown, about 3 minutes per side. Transfer to the plate to drain and immediately sprinkle with a small pinch of salt. Repeat with the remaining mushrooms.

**SERVE:** Fill each tortilla with a fried mushroom strip and some of the pickled cabbage. Top with the spicy mayo and salsa brava and garnish with the cilantro. Serve with lime wedges.

# AL PASTOR MADRE TACOS

## MAKES 8 TACOS

2 teaspoons extra-virgin olive oil

2 cups Mushroom Pastor (page 213)

8 Tortillas (page 209), or store-bought corn tortillas, warmed

4 pineapple rings, cut in half (or 1 cup diced fresh pineapple)

¼ cup chopped fresh cilantro

¼ cup chopped onion

¼ cup Salsa Negra (page 196)

1 cup Guacamole (page 41)

Lime or lemon wedges, for serving

In a medium nonstick pan over medium heat, heat the oil. Add the mushrooms and cook until just warmed through, about 5 minutes.

Divide the warm mushrooms among the warmed tortillas. Place the pineapple next to the mushrooms and top with the cilantro, onion, and salsa. Serve with the guacamole and lime wedges on the side.

# JACKFRUIT MIXIOTE MADRE TACOS

MAKES 8 TACOS

Canola, rice bran, or other neutral oil, for frying

1 small onion, thinly sliced, rings broken up

8 Tortillas (page 209), or store-bought corn tortillas, warmed

2 cups Jackfruit Mixiote (page 211)

2 cups Quick-Pickled Cabbage (page 131)

½ cup Cashew Crema (page 184)

½ cup chopped fresh cilantro

Line a plate with paper towels. In a large nonstick or cast-iron pan over medium-high heat, heat about ½ inch of oil to 350°F. Add the onions and fry just until golden, 1 to 2 minutes. Transfer to the paper towel–lined plate to drain.

Fill each tortilla with some of the jackfruit and top with the pickled cabbage and crispy onions. Garnish with the cashew crema and cilantro.

# ALBÓNDIGAS MADRE TACOS

## MAKES 6 TACOS

Canola, rice bran, or other neutral oil, for frying

1 cup rice flour

1 tablespoon Himalayan salt

1 onion, halved and thinly sliced

1 recipe Black Bean Burger mixture (page 90)

6 Tortillas (page 209), or store-bought corn tortillas, warmed

¾ cup Salsa Roja (page 190)

½ cup Cashew Crema (page 184)

Hot sauce, to taste

2 tablespoons chopped fresh cilantro

In a heavy-bottomed, high-sided frying pan over medium-high heat, heat about 2 inches of oil to 350°F. Line a plate or baking sheet with a few layers of paper towels and place nearby for draining.

In a medium bowl, whisk together the rice flour and salt. Use your hands to break up the sliced onions over the bowl and toss in the flour mixture to coat completely. Use a slotted spoon or tongs to lift the onions out of the flour mixture and shake off any excess. Fry the onions until they're crisp and golden, 2 to 3 minutes. Transfer to the plate to drain.

Use a melon baller or soup spoon to form 18 meatballs from the black bean mixture (they should be about 2 tablespoons each). Working in batches so as not to crowd the pan, fry the meatballs for about 2 minutes per side and transfer to the plate to drain. Repeat with the remaining meatballs.

On each tortilla, place 3 of the meatballs and spoon the salsa roja on top. Drizzle the cashew crema over the meatballs, add hot sauce, and top with the crispy fried onions. Garnish with the cilantro.

# COCONUT MADRE TACOS

## MAKES 8 TACOS

### FOR THE MEXICAN KIMCHI

½ red cabbage, cored and very thinly sliced

One 4-inch piece fresh ginger, cut into 1-inch chunks

2 whole dried guajillo chiles

**(INGREDIENTS AND RECIPE CONTINUE)**

3 jalapeños, stemmed and sliced

7 garlic cloves

10 cilantro stems

3 tablespoons Himalayan salt

1 tablespoon coriander seeds

## FOR THE COCONUT TACOS

1 pound sliced young coconut meat
(thawed if frozen)

1 cup fresh lime juice

2 tablespoons Old Bay seasoning

1 teaspoon Himalayan salt

1 teaspoon ground cumin

1 teaspoon freshly ground black pepper

2 cups all-purpose flour

1 (12-ounce) bottle JUST Egg, or
1½ cups liquid egg replacer

3 cups panko breadcrumbs

Canola, rice bran, or other neutral oil, for
frying

8 Tortillas (page 209), or store-bought
corn tortillas, warmed

½ cup chopped fresh cilantro

2 limes, cut into wedges

## FOR THE CARROT MAYONNAISE

2 small yellow carrots, peeled and cut
into 2-inch pieces

1 cup vegan mayonnaise

1 teaspoon apple cider vinegar

½ teaspoon Himalayan salt

**MAKE THE MEXICAN KIMCHI:** In a
pickling crock or large, wide-mouth
jar, add the cabbage, ginger, guajillos,
jalapeños, garlic, cilantro stems, salt,
coriander, and just enough water to
cover. Tap the jar a few times to release
any trapped air bubbles. (You can
also use a chopstick or the handle of a
wooden spoon to ease out some of the
bubbles.) Place a weight on top of the
mixture to keep it submerged in the
water. Seal the crock and let it sit at
room temperature for at least 5 days.

**MAKE THE COCONUT TACOS:** In a large
bowl, add the coconut, lime juice, Old
Bay, salt, cumin, and pepper and stir to
combine. Cover and refrigerate for at
least 8 hours and up to overnight.

Set three wide, shallow bowls next
to one another. Add the flour to one,
the egg replacer to the next, and the
breadcrumbs in the last bowl.

In a heavy-bottomed, high-sided frying pan over medium-high heat, heat about 2 inches of oil to 350°F. Line a plate or baking sheet with a few layers of paper towels and place nearby for draining.

Drain the marinated coconut. Working in batches, add some of the coconut to the flour and shake off any excess. Dip the coconut in the egg replacer, followed by the breadcrumbs. Fry the marinated coconut just until golden, 1 minute. Using a skimmer or slotted spoon, transfer the coconut to the plate and repeat with the remaining coconut.

**MAKE THE CARROT MAYONNAISE:** In a medium saucepan over medium-high heat, bring 4 cups of water to a boil. Add the carrots and cook until just tender, about 5 minutes. Transfer to an ice bath.

In a high-speed blender, add the carrots, vegan mayo, vinegar, and salt and blend until smooth. Taste and adjust the seasoning.

**ASSEMBLE THE TACOS:** Fill each tortilla with some of the crispy coconut, a tablespoon or two of the kimchi, and a drizzle of the mayo. Finish with the cilantro and serve with the lime wedges.

# MUSHROOM FAJITAS

While we take pride in sharing traditional Mexican culinary preparations, we're also a California restaurant. So we wanted to devote space on our menu to the Mexican-*inspired* dishes that people in the States have come to love. These fajitas are the perfect example—they're a Tex-Mex hybrid, combining sizzling-hot veggies in soft, warm tortillas with all the fixings, like guac, cashew crema, pico de gallo, and black beans. It comes as no surprise to us that this is one of our most popular dishes.

SERVES 4

## FOR THE MUSHROOM FAJITAS

2 portobello mushroom caps, stems removed and sliced ½-inch thick

¼ cup extra-virgin olive oil

1 garlic clove, minced

1½ teaspoons Himalayan salt

4 medium onions, thinly sliced

2 teaspoons dried oregano

1 bay leaf

2 poblano peppers, stemmed, seeded, and thinly sliced

1 red bell pepper, stemmed, seeded, and thinly sliced

2 teaspoons apple cider vinegar

## FOR SERVING

12 flour tortillas, warmed

2 cups shredded romaine lettuce

1½ cups Pico de Gallo (page 194)

1 cup Guacamole (page 41)

½ cup Cashew Crema (page 184)

Black Beans (page 221), optional

**Make the fajitas:** Preheat the oven to 350°F. Line a baking sheet with parchment.

(RECIPE CONTINUES)

In a medium bowl, add the mushrooms, 1 tablespoon of the oil, the garlic, and ½ teaspoon of the salt and toss to coat. Line up the sliced mushrooms on the baking sheet and bake for 10 minutes.

In a large nonstick or cast-iron pan over medium-high heat, heat the remaining 3 tablespoons oil. Add the onions, oregano, bay leaf, and ½ teaspoon of the salt and cook, stirring, until the onions have collapsed and begun to caramelize, about 15 minutes. Add the poblanos, bell pepper, vinegar, and the remaining ½ teaspoon salt and cook until the peppers are very soft and caramelized, about 10 minutes. Add the baked mushrooms and toss to incorporate.

**Serve:** Fill the tortillas with the mushroom fajitas and top as desired with the lettuce, pico de gallo, guacamole, and cashew crema. Serve with black beans, if it sounds tasty.

# PLANTAIN MOLOTES WITH MOLE NEGRO

Molotes are essentially like little savory plantain dumplings that are filled with vegan chorizo, fried, and served with mole. It's a classic nighttime street-food recipe from the Istmo region of Oaxaca, a part of Mexico that has taken on a lot of the Caribbean food influences that have traveled up from Central America.

SERVES 4

## FOR THE MOLOTES

4 plantains (firm to the touch, some black spots are fine)

⅔ cup rice flour

2 teaspoons Himalayan salt

1 cup vegan chorizo, crumbled if needed

Canola, rice bran, or other neutral oil, for frying

## FOR SERVING

1 cup Mole Negro (page 200), warmed

¼ cup Cashew Crema (page 184)

¼ cup Almond Cotija (page 183)

2 tablespoons roughly chopped fresh mint leaves

**Make the molotes:** Preheat the oven to 350°F. Line a baking sheet with parchment.

In each plantain, make 3 small slits in the skin to help the steam escape. Line the plantains up on the baking sheet and bake until the flesh is soft but not mushy, 12 to 15 minutes. Let the plantains cool completely before peeling.

(RECIPE CONTINUES)

Working over a large bowl, peel and roughly break up the cooled plantains. Use a potato masher to mash the plantains into a fairly smooth pulp. Add the flour and salt and mix with a wooden spoon or spatula to combine. Place about ⅓ cup of the mixture on a square of parchment or plastic and spread it into about a 4-inch circle. Add about 2 tablespoons of the chorizo to the center and fold the sides of the parchment up to close the plantain mixture around the chorizo. Use your hands to finish forming the molote into a croquette shape, making sure the chorizo is sealed inside. Repeat with the remaining ingredients. Transfer the molotes to a plate or tray.

In a heavy-bottomed, high-sided frying pan over medium-high heat, heat about 2 inches of oil to 350°F. Line a baking sheet with a few layers of paper towels and place nearby for draining.

Add two or three molotes to the hot oil, depending on the size of your pan, and fry until golden brown, 2 to 3 minutes per side. Transfer to the baking sheet to drain. Repeat until all the molotes have been cooked.

**Serve:** Spread the mole on the bottom of a large serving plate. Arrange the molotes on top and finish with the crema, almond cotija, and mint.

# FLAUTAS DE HIBISCUS

When we started serving hibiscus tea, we noticed that we were throwing away a lot of leftover dried hibiscus flowers—and food waste is not something we're about. We also knew that in some regions in Mexico, you see people serving hibiscus flowers in tortas and various desserts. With a little experimentation, we figured out that if you balance hibiscus's floral flavor with vinegar and sugar, you get a product that's satisfyingly meaty with a great chewy texture. So now all those flowers make the perfect filling for our flautas, or fried rolled-up tortilla "cigars," which get draped in guacamole, cashew nacho cheese, pumpkin seed parm, and pico de gallo.

SERVES 4

### FOR THE FLAUTAS

1 cup dried hibiscus flowers

1 tablespoon extra-virgin olive oil

2 medium onions, chopped

1 teaspoon Himalayan salt

1 cup grated carrots

1 cup grated jicama

1 tablespoon sugar

1 teaspoon apple cider vinegar

½ teaspoon chopped fresh
   thyme leaves

Canola, rice bran, or other
   neutral oil, for frying

12 Tortillas (page 209), or store-
   bought corn tortillas

### FOR SERVING

½ cup Salsa Verde (page 191)

½ cup Cashew Nacho Cheese
   (page 181)

½ cup Pico de Gallo (page 194)

½ cup Guacamole (page 41)

¼ cup Pumpkin Seed Parmesan
   (page 182)

¼ cup chopped fresh cilantro

(RECIPE CONTINUES)

**Make the flautas:** In a medium saucepan over medium-high heat, add the hibiscus flowers and 4 cups of water. Bring to a boil, reduce the heat to low, and simmer, covered, for 5 minutes. Remove from the heat and let sit for 10 minutes. Drain and set aside. (You can also reserve the resulting hibiscus tea, sweeten to taste with agave or sugar, and store in the fridge.)

In a large nonstick pan over medium-high heat, heat the olive oil. Add the onion and ¼ teaspoon of the salt and cook, stirring, until translucent, about 8 minutes. Add the carrot and jicama and continue cooking until the carrot has softened slightly, about 5 minutes. Add the hibiscus flowers and cook for another 5 minutes. Add the sugar, vinegar, thyme, and the remaining ¾ teaspoon salt and stir to combine.

In a Dutch oven, heavy-bottomed pot, or high-sided frying pan over medium-high heat, heat about 3 inches of canola oil to 350°F. Line a plate or baking sheet with a few layers of paper towels and place nearby for draining.

Place about ¼ cup of the hibiscus filling in each tortilla. Roll up the tortilla into a long tube shape and secure with a toothpick. Working in batches, fry the flautas until golden, 2 to 3 minutes. Transfer to the plate and repeat with the remaining flautas.

Serve the flautas with the salsa verde, nacho cheese, pico de gallo, and guacamole for dipping. Alternatively, you can layer them on top of the flautas and serve family-style. Garnish with the pumpkin seed parmesan and cilantro.

# ENCHILADAS VERDES

There's not much more to say about these hearty, saucy go-tos—which are just as loved here in the States as they are across Mexico—other than that we offer this veggie-forward version with potatoes and peas, but this recipe is a great canvas for pretty much all the Madre fillings in this book.

SERVES 4

1 pound potatoes, peeled and quartered (about 2½ cups)

Himalayan salt, to taste

1 tablespoon extra-virgin olive oil

1 cup diced onion

2 garlic cloves, minced

½ cup peas, fresh or frozen and thawed

½ small jalapeño, stemmed, seeded, and minced

½ teaspoon chili powder

8 Tortillas (page 209), or store-bought corn tortillas, warmed

2 cups Salsa Verde (page 191)

½ cup pumpkin seeds, toasted until fragrant

¼ cup chopped fresh cilantro

1 avocado, sliced

2 cups Black Beans (page 221), warmed

Preheat the oven to 400°F.

In a large pot over medium-high heat, add the potatoes, enough water to cover, and a generous pinch of salt. Bring to a boil and cook until the potatoes are cooked through, about 10 minutes. Drain and let cool slightly. Dice the cooked potatoes into ½-inch pieces.

In a large nonstick or cast-iron pan over medium-high heat, heat the oil. Add the onion, garlic, and a pinch of salt and cook until the onion

(RECIPE CONTINUES)

is translucent, about 7 minutes. Add the potatoes, peas, jalapeño, chili powder, and salt to taste and cook until the jalapeño has softened and the potatoes start to coat the mixture, 5 more minutes. Taste and adjust salt if needed.

In a small baking dish, pour about ½ cup of the salsa verde and spread it around to coat the bottom. Fill each tortilla with about ¼ cup of the potato mixture, roll it up, and place it seam side down in the dish. Repeat with the remaining tortillas, lining them up snugly in the dish. Spread the remaining salsa verde on top of the enchiladas. Bake until the salsa bubbles and the edges of the tortillas begin to crisp slightly, about 20 minutes.

Garnish with the pumpkin seeds and cilantro and serve with the avocado and black beans.

# TLAYUDAS

Tlayudas are the iconic dish of Oaxaca, and you can find them offered both by street vendors and in restaurants. They're large tortillas that have been warmed on a comal or charred on a grill (though a sauté pan on the stove works just fine), then topped with all manner of toppings: traditionally a base of refried beans along with cabbage, avocado, some kind of meat, plus cheese and salsa. Our version doesn't stray too far from the original, calling for our creamy house black beans, spicy mushroom pastor, and a liberal drizzle of salsa roja.

SERVES 4

1½ cups sunflower seeds

2 tablespoons extra-virgin olive oil

2 garlic cloves, chopped

1 teaspoon Himalayan salt

4 Tortillas (page 209), or store-bought large flour tortillas, 12 to 16 inches in diameter

1 cup Black Beans (page 221)

⅛ cup chopped cilantro, optional

2 cups shredded vegan mozzarella cheese

2 cups thinly shredded red cabbage

2 cups Mushroom Pastor (page 213)

2 avocados, sliced

1 cup Salsa Roja (page 190)

In a medium bowl, add the sunflower seeds and enough water to cover. Soak for 30 minutes and drain well.

In a large nonstick pan over medium heat, heat the oil. Add the soaked sunflower seeds, garlic, and salt and gently cook until just fragrant and beginning to brown, 3 to 5 minutes.

(RECIPE CONTINUES)

Transfer the sunflower seed mixture to a food processor and process until smooth. Add a teaspoon or two of water to loosen the mixture if needed.

Return the same pan to medium heat. Spread a few tablespoons of the sunflower butter on a tortilla, then transfer it to the hot pan. Add a layer each of the beans, cilantro (if using), cheese, cabbage, and mushroom pastor. Cook, shaking the pan occasionally, until the tortilla is crisp and the cheese has melted, about 5 minutes. Fold the tortilla in half and cook for another minute.

Slide the tlayuda onto a cutting board and tuck in the avocado slices and a few tablespoons of the salsa. Repeat with the remaining tortillas. Cut the tlayudas in half and serve in wedges.

CHAPTER 5

DULCES

# MEXICAN WEDDING COOKIES

We're not sure how exactly these became "wedding cookies" (maybe because they're elegantly draped in white?), but we do know that these soft, nutty, buttery (and yet not buttery) confections are the perfect sweet bits, and especially delicious crumbled over our ice creams.

MAKES ABOUT 28 COOKIES

1 cup melted coconut oil

½ cup powdered sugar, plus
   more for dusting

2 cups all-purpose flour

1 cup chopped pecans

1 tablespoon vanilla extract

½ teaspoon Himalayan salt

Preheat the oven to 350°F. Line two baking sheets with parchment.

In the bowl of a stand mixer fitted with the paddle attachment, add the coconut oil and powdered sugar and beat at medium speed until thoroughly combined, about 3 minutes. Add the flour, pecans, vanilla, and salt and mix on low speed until the flour is incorporated. Increase the speed to medium and beat until the mixture is fluffy and well mixed, about 5 minutes.

Scoop the dough out in rounded tablespoons onto the prepared baking sheets. Using your hands, gently flatten the cookies to about ½ inch thick. Chill the cookies for about 10 minutes before baking.

Bake for 10 minutes, rotate the pans, and bake for another 10 minutes, or until the cookies are just beginning to look golden around the edges. Let cool for a few minutes on the pan, then transfer the cookies to a wire rack to cool completely.

Spoon a few tablespoons of powdered sugar into a bowl. Gently coat the cooled cookies in the powdered sugar, adding more sugar to the bowl as needed.

# CHURROS

It's pretty hard to beat a bag of still-warm churros (a.k.a. fried dough that's been tossed with cinnamon and sugar) that you bought from a street cart, but these come pretty close. Especially because you can eat them fresh out of the fryer and drizzled with chipotle-spiked Mexican chocolate sauce.

MAKES ABOUT 12 CHURROS

## FOR THE CHOCOLATE CINNAMON SAUCE

¾ cup semisweet chocolate (about 6 ounces)

½ cup Cashew Crema (page 184)

1 teaspoon ground cinnamon

⅛ teaspoon chipotle powder

⅛ teaspoon Himalayan salt

## FOR THE CHURROS

2 cups all-purpose flour

½ cup packed brown sugar

1 tablespoon ground cinnamon

4 teaspoons canola, rice bran, or other neutral oil, plus more for frying

2 teaspoons sugar

½ teaspoon Himalayan salt

2 teaspoons egg replacer, mixed with 2 tablespoons cold water

**Make the chocolate sauce:** In a medium saucepan over medium-high heat, bring about 1 inch of water to a simmer. Place the chocolate in a heat-safe bowl and place the bowl over the pan. Melt the chocolate, stirring occasionally, to evenly distribute the heat. Once the chocolate is nearly melted, remove the bowl from the pan and continue stirring to melt the remaining chocolate. Add the cashew crema and whisk until

(RECIPE CONTINUES)

smooth and combined. Add the cinnamon, chipotle powder, and salt and whisk once more. Set aside while you make the churros. (If needed, you can warm up the sauce for 1 minute over the warm water in the same pot.)

**Make the churros:** Place the flour in a large bowl and set aside. On a large plate, add the brown sugar and cinnamon and mix with a fork. Set aside.

In a small saucepan over medium-high heat, add the oil, sugar, salt, and 1½ cups of water and whisk to combine. Bring to a boil and immediately pour over the flour. Using a spatula or wooden spoon, mix until smooth and any lumps have dissolved. Add the egg replacer and mix again until smooth.

In a heavy-bottomed, high-sided frying pan over medium-high heat, heat about 2 inches of oil to 350°F. Line a plate or baking sheet with a few layers of paper towels and place nearby for draining.

Add the flour mixture to a pastry bag with a star tip. Working in batches so as not to crowd the pan, squeeze 4-inch strips of dough into the hot oil. Fry the churros, turning occasionally, until deep golden brown, 5 to 7 minutes. Transfer the churros to a plate to cool for just a minute, then roll in the brown sugar–cinnamon mixture. Repeat with the remaining dough.

Serve the warm, crisp churros with the chocolate sauce for dipping.

# COFFEE FLAN

We wear it as a badge of honor that we can serve up our plant-based version of this hallmark dessert that's so beloved in Mexico, and that it's still every bit as creamy and luscious as the original (thanks to agar powder, which is derived from algae). As if that weren't sumptuous enough, we steep coffee beans overnight in the coconut milk base and top the whole thing off with homemade caramel.

SERVES 6

4 cups full-fat coconut milk

½ cup whole coffee beans

1¼ cups raw cashews

¼ cup sugar

½ cup agave nectar

2 ounces espresso
   (one standard shot)

1 vanilla bean, seeds scraped

½ teaspoon Himalayan salt

½ teaspoon agar powder

In a large jar or covered bowl, soak the coconut milk and the coffee beans together overnight. With a slotted spoon, remove the coffee beans and discard, reserving the infused coconut milk.

Place six 8-ounce ramekins on a baking sheet and set aside.

In a medium sauté pan, add the cashews. Set the pan over low heat and toast the nuts, tossing or stirring frequently, until just fragrant and beginning to turn golden, about 10 minutes.

In a small saucepan over medium-high heat, add the toasted cashews and enough water to cover. Bring to a boil, immediately remove from the heat, drain the cashews, and set aside.

(RECIPE CONTINUES)

In a small saucepan over medium-low heat, add the sugar, making sure it's in an even layer. Without stirring, heat until the sugar dissolves completely and turns a medium caramel color, about 7 minutes. Quickly distribute the caramel into the bottoms of the six ramekins.

In the pitcher of a high-speed blender, add the drained cashews, agave, espresso, vanilla seeds, salt, and half of the infused coconut milk. Blend until smooth.

In a small saucepan over medium-high heat, whisk together the other half of the infused coconut milk and the agar powder. Bring to a gentle simmer, reduce the heat to low, and cook for about 5 minutes. Add the mixture to the blender and blend once more for a few seconds to completely combine.

Carefully pour the mixture into the ramekins and chill for at least 6 hours to set. To serve, run a knife around the inside of the ramekin and carefully invert the ramekin onto a plate.

# TIRAMISU CON MEZCAL

Tiramisu may not be the first dessert you think of in a Mexican restaurant—much less a vegan one—but our distinctly modernized version with smoky mezcal and Mexican espresso gives the Italians a run for their money.

SERVES 6

8 ounces soft tofu

¼ cup unsweetened almond milk

¼ cup agave nectar

1½ tablespoons peanut butter

1 tablespoon vanilla extract

¼ teaspoon Himalayan salt

1 cup espresso or very strong brewed coffee

1 ounce mezcal

8 ounces vegan ladyfingers

2 tablespoons Mexican cocoa powder

In a high-speed blender, add the tofu, almond milk, agave, peanut butter, vanilla, and salt and blend until very smooth.

In a medium bowl, add the espresso and mezcal and stir to combine.

Dip the ladyfingers briefly in the coffee mixture, just a second or two on each side. Line the base of an 8 × 8-inch baking dish with a layer of the soaked ladyfingers. Add a layer of the tofu mixture (about half), using a spatula or knife to smooth the top. Repeat with another layer of soaked ladyfingers, followed by the remaining tofu mixture. Sift the cocoa powder in an even layer over the top. Cover and chill for 2 hours before serving.

# HELADOS

We get it—desserts are better with a scoop of ice cream. So we offer a handful of simple flavors to make any of our sweet offerings à la mode, or to just scoop into a bowl. Our coconut milk base yields a lusciously smooth texture that we can infuse with things like classic vanilla bean or piloncillo, a raw cane sugar with a unique sweet and smoky flavor. You can find it formed into cones in most Mexican grocery stores; you just have to soften it with hot water. Also on the menu are Mexican chocolate and sweet, floral passionfruit.

## MEXICAN CHOCOLATE

MAKES 4 CUPS

1½ ounces stone-ground dark Mexican chocolate

2 (13.5-ounce) cans full-fat coconut milk (about 3⅓ cups)

½ cup agave nectar

¾ teaspoon Himalayan salt

½ teaspoon vanilla extract

½ teaspoon guar gum

In a high-speed blender, add the chocolate and about 1 cup of the coconut milk. Blend until the chocolate has broken down and the mixture is nearly smooth. Add the remaining 2 cups coconut milk, the agave, salt, vanilla, and guar gum and blend until smooth. Cover and chill for at least 4 hours or overnight. Freeze in an ice-cream maker according to the manufacturer's instructions. Serve right away or store in an airtight container in the freezer.

## PASSIONFRUIT

MAKES 4 CUPS

2 (13.5-ounce) cans full-fat coconut milk (about 3⅓ cups)

¾ cup agave nectar

½ cup passionfruit pulp (strained if using fresh passionfruit)

1¼ teaspoons Himalayan salt

1 teaspoon vanilla extract

1 teaspoon guar gum

In a high-speed blender, add the coconut milk, agave, passionfruit pulp, salt, vanilla, and guar gum and blend until smooth. Cover and chill for at least 4 hours or overnight. Freeze in an ice-cream maker according to the manufacturer's instructions. Serve right away or store in an airtight container in the freezer.

# PILONCILLO

MAKES 4 CUPS

2½ cups boiling water

4 ounces piloncillo (can use 1-ounce or 2-ounce cones)

½ can full-fat coconut milk (a little more than ¾ cup)

2 teaspoons vanilla extract

1½ teaspoons guar gum

1½ teaspoons Himalayan salt

In a medium bowl, add the hot water and piloncillo. Stirring occasionally to help the piloncillo dissolve, let the mixture sit until the piloncillo is completely dissolved and the water is lukewarm.

In a high-speed blender, add the piloncillo mixture, coconut milk,

vanilla, guar gum, and salt and blend until smooth. Cover and chill overnight. Freeze in an ice-cream maker according to the manufacturer's instructions. Serve right away or store in an airtight container in the freezer.

# COCONUT VANILLA BEAN

MAKES 4 CUPS

2 (13.5-ounce) cans full-fat coconut milk (about 3⅓ cups)

¼ cup plus 2 tablespoons agave nectar

1 vanilla bean, seeds scraped

½ teaspoon Himalayan salt

½ teaspoon guar gum

In a high-speed blender, add the coconut milk, agave, vanilla seeds, salt, and guar gum and blend until smooth. Cover and chill overnight. Freeze in an ice-cream maker according to the manufacturer's instructions. Serve right away or store in an airtight container in the freezer.

HELADOS

# FUDGE BROWNIES WITH SALTED MEZCAL CARAMEL SAUCE AND CASHEW WHIPPED CREAM

Brownies are just as beloved in Mexico as they are here in the States, so it only made sense that we offer this gooey, chocolatey dessert on our menu. The secret ingredient—fittingly—is avocado, which lends the brownies a rich, unctuous texture that you'd normally get from eggs. Then we dress the whole thing up with a mezcal-based caramel and a cashew whipped cream. And if you really want to blow some minds, you can finish it off with a sprinkling of coconut bacon.

MAKES 9 BROWNIES

### FOR THE BROWNIES

⅓ cup coconut oil, melted and cooled, plus more for the pan

2¾ cups all-purpose flour

½ cup cocoa powder

1 teaspoon baking powder

1 teaspoon baking soda

¼ teaspoon Himalayan salt

1 ripe avocado, mashed

1¾ cups packed brown sugar

¼ cup canola or other neutral oil

1 shot espresso

2 tablespoons apple cider vinegar

2 teaspoons vanilla extract

### FOR THE CASHEW WHIPPED CREAM

1 cup cashews

¼ cup cane sugar

¼ teaspoon Himalayan salt

½ cup coconut oil

## FOR THE SALTED MEZCAL CARAMEL SAUCE

1 cup agave nectar

¼ cup mezcal

¼ teaspoon Himalayan salt

## FOR SERVING

Coconut Bacon (page 223), optional

(RECIPE CONTINUES)

Preheat the oven to 350°F. Line a 9 × 9-inch baking dish with parchment and grease the dish and the parchment with a small amount of coconut oil.

In a medium bowl, add the flour, cocoa powder, baking powder, baking soda, and salt. Mix with a fork to combine.

In a high-speed blender, add the avocado, brown sugar, coconut oil, canola oil, espresso, vinegar, and vanilla and blend until smooth. Add about a third of the dry ingredient mixture and blend on low speed to incorporate. Repeat twice more with the remaining dry ingredients.

Pour the brownie batter into the pan and smooth the top with a spatula. Bake until a toothpick or cake tester comes out with just a few crumbs, 20 to 25 minutes. Let cool for at least 20 minutes before serving.

**Make the cashew whipped cream:** In a high-speed blender, add the cashews, sugar, salt, and 1½ cups of water and blend until smooth and creamy. Add the coconut oil and continue blending until the mixture is completely combined. Transfer to the bowl of a stand mixer fitted with the whisk attachment. Whip until fluffy, about 5 minutes.

**Make the caramel sauce:** In a small saucepan over medium-high heat, add the agave and mezcal. Bring to a simmer and reduce the heat to medium-low. Let the mixture reduce to a medium amber color, about 30 minutes, until all the alcohol has cooked off. Remove from the heat and stir in the salt. Let cool for 15 minutes before serving.

**Serve:** Cut the brownies into squares and serve with a dollop of the cashew whipped cream and a drizzle of the caramel sauce. Sprinkle with a bit of coconut bacon, if using.

This recipe also works well in round mini cake or muffin molds to produce individual portions.

# PINEAPPLE UPSIDE-DOWN CAKE

There's really nothing that compares to the deep sweetness of pineapple when it's baked, especially when it's baked into a rich vegan cake and topped with vanilla bean ice cream and salted mezcal caramel sauce. And yet, despite its (very) decadent consistency and flavor profile, the pineapple keeps things feeling as refreshing as a cocktail on a Oaxacan beach.

SERVES 8

½ cup melted coconut oil, plus more for the pan

1 pineapple, peeled, cored, and cut into ¼-inch rings

1½ cups all-purpose flour

1 cup sugar

1½ tablespoons egg replacer

2 teaspoons baking powder

1 teaspoon baking soda

¾ teaspoon Himalayan salt

¼ cup plus 2 tablespoons unsweetened almond milk

¼ cup fresh pineapple juice

¼ cup coconut or nondairy yogurt

½ teaspoon vanilla extract

1 recipe Coconut Vanilla Bean Ice Cream (page 165), for serving

1 recipe Salted Mezcal Caramel Sauce (page 169), for serving

Preheat the oven to 350°F. Grease a 9-inch cake pan or eight nonstick mini Bundt pans with a small amount of coconut oil. If using the 9-inch pan, line with a circle of parchment, and grease the parchment.

If using the 9-inch pan, arrange as many pineapple rings (either whole or cut into halves or quarters, to fit more fruit) as will fit on the bottom of the cake pan in one layer. If using the mini Bundt pans, place one full ring in the bottom of each pan.

(RECIPE CONTINUES)

In the bowl of a stand mixer fitted with the paddle attachment, add the flour, sugar, egg replacer, baking powder, baking soda, and salt. Mix on low speed briefly to combine. Add the almond milk, pineapple juice, yogurt, and vanilla and mix on medium speed until the batter is light, fluffy, and fully combined, about 3 minutes.

Pour the batter into the prepared cake pan or mini Bundts, being careful not to disturb the layer of pineapple. (If you are using the mini Bundts, make sure to leave at least ¼ inch of space at the top of the molds for the cakes to expand as they cook.) Smooth the top of the batter with a spatula and bake until the cake is fully set and a toothpick or cake tester comes out clean, 30 to 35 minutes if using the mini Bundts or 35 to 40 minutes if using the 9-inch pan.

Set the cake pan(s) on a wire rack and let cool until just warm to the touch. Place a large plate over the cake pan(s) and invert onto the plate. Remove the parchment, if using.

Serve with a scoop of the vanilla ice cream and a drizzle of the salted mezcal caramel sauce.

CHAPTER 6

# QUESOS &
# CREMAS

# SPICY MAYO

A spiced, creamy spread that can stand in for mayo or sour cream.

1 cup vegan mayonnaise

½ teaspoon minced garlic

2 teaspoons Salsa Negra
   (page 196)

2 teaspoons fresh lemon juice

½ teaspoon Himalayan salt, plus
   more to taste

In a medium bowl, whisk together the mayonnaise, garlic, hot sauce, lemon juice, and salt until smooth and combined. Taste and adjust the seasoning.

# CASHEW QUESO BLANCO

We formulated this recipe to emulate the mild white fresh cheese you find on pretty much every popular Mexican dish.

MAKES ABOUT 2 CUPS

2 cups raw cashews

3 tablespoons fresh lemon juice

2 tablespoons nutritional yeast

1½ teaspoons Himalayan salt

In a high-speed blender, add the cashews, lemon juice, nutritional yeast, salt, and ½ cup of water. Pulse until a chunky paste forms. Cover and refrigerate for at least 30 minutes before using.

# CASHEW NACHO CHEESE

Not much more needs to be said here, other than make a batch; spread and dip liberally.

MAKES 3 CUPS

1 cup raw cashews, soaked for 4 hours or up to overnight

2 tablespoons pumpkin seeds

2 tablespoons fresh lemon juice

1 small garlic clove

½ to 1 whole jalapeño, seeded

2 teaspoons Himalayan salt, plus more to taste

1½ teaspoons chipotle powder

Drain and rinse the cashews under cold water until the water runs clear. Transfer the cashews to a high-speed blender and add the pumpkin seeds, lemon juice, garlic, jalapeño, salt, chipotle powder, and 1¼ cups of water. Blend until smooth and creamy. The mixture will keep in the fridge, covered, for 3 to 4 days.

# PUMPKIN SEED PARMESAN

This cheese/condiment can really bring together a dish as a finishing touch, thanks to its subtle saltiness and spice.

MAKES 1 CUP

½ cup pumpkin seeds, toasted
    until fragrant

½ cup sesame seeds, toasted
    until fragrant

1 teaspoon Himalayan salt

½ teaspoon minced garlic

½ teaspoon chili powder

In a food processor or high-speed blender, add the pumpkin seeds, sesame seeds, salt, garlic, and chili powder and pulse until a loose powder forms. Store in the refrigerator for up to 2 weeks.

# ALMOND COTIJA

Aslightly tangier alternative to Cashew Queso Blanco (page 178). Together they're excellent costars for finishing sprinkles.

MAKES ABOUT 2 CUPS

1½ cups blanched almonds

¼ teaspoon dulse flakes or granules

2 tablespoons fresh lemon juice

1 teaspoon Himalayan salt, plus more to taste

Place the almonds in a large, dry nonstick or cast-iron pan. Place the pan over medium-low heat and toast, shaking the pan frequently, until the almonds are just fragrant, 8 to 10 minutes. Transfer the almonds to a plate to cool completely.

In a food processor, add the cooled toasted almonds and the dulse and process until finely ground. Add the lemon juice and salt and process briefly to combine. Taste and adjust the seasoning. Store in an airtight jar for up to 1 week.

# CASHEW CREMA

The perfect sour cream substitute—tangy, creamy, and ideal for drizzling on just about everything.

MAKES 1 CUP

½ cup raw cashews, soaked for 2 hours or up to 12 hours

2 tablespoons fresh lemon juice

½ teaspoon Himalayan salt

Drain and rinse the cashews under cold water until the water runs clear. Transfer the cashews to a high-speed blender and add the lemon juice, salt, and ½ cup water. Blend until smooth and creamy. Refrigerate in an airtight container for up to 5 days.

CHAPTER 7

# SALSAS & MOLES

# THE GRACIAS MADRE GUIDE
## TO SALSA CHILES

The recipes in this section call for an assortment of dried chiles, which are what give these salsas—and any other sauce or dish that uses them—their signature heat, smokiness, and flavor. Many of them can be easy to come by in grocery stores, especially Mexican markets, or can be ordered online.

**ANCHO CHILES:** These sweet and smoky peppers made from dried poblanos are one of the most common chiles you'll find in Mexican cooking and have mild to medium heat.

**ARBOL CHILES:** The chile de árbol ("chile of the tree") is small but mighty, packing intense heat. It's one of the most common chiles used to make the "fried" salsas—salsas where the ingredients have been rapidly cooked down until they're soft—that you find on the table in taquerías.

**CASCABEL CHILES**: These don't contribute a lot of heat compared to other chiles, but where they shine is their earthy, slightly tobacco-like smokiness.

**CHILHUACLE CHILES:** Meaning "old chile" in Nahuatl (the language of the Aztecs) and found primarily in Oaxaca, the chilhuacle is a dark, moody chile that gives signature deep flavor and color to mole negro. They're largely grown in southern Mexico and can be more difficult to find than other varieties, which is why we recommend substituting cascabel chiles in the event they're not available to you.

**GUAJILLO CHILES:** After anchos, these are some of the most popular chiles in Mexico and give the signature deep red color to Mexican stews. They have an interesting fruity flavor with medium heat.

**MORITA CHILES:** Like chipotle peppers, these are made from smoked red jalapeños, but moritas are smaller and spicier. Their heat isn't too aggressive, though, which lets their fruitiness come through.

**PASILLA CHILES:** These guys have a deep, rich sweetness, almost like a raisin, along with heat that can range from mild to hot (but not too crazy). But what makes them special is their meaty texture that helps thicken salsas and other sauces.

# SALSA ROJA

Your classic dip-the-chips salsa. While red salsa can be raw or cooked, we prefer to char the tomatoes in order to deepen their flavor.

MAKES ABOUT 2 CUPS

10 Roma or plum tomatoes

1 medium onion, quartered

4 garlic cloves

4 dried guajillo chiles

Himalayan salt, to taste

Add the tomatoes, onion, and garlic to a dry cast-iron pan. Place the pan over medium heat and toast the vegetables until deeply charred, 15 to 20 minutes. Add the chiles to the pan and toast briefly, about 2 more minutes. Transfer to a high-speed blender, add a pinch of salt, and blend until smooth. Taste and adjust the seasoning. Store in a sealed container in the refrigerator for up to 1 week.

# SALSA VERDE

Fresh, green tomatillos give this raw salsa an equally fresh, green flavor that complements cooked red salsas.

MAKES ABOUT 3 CUPS

8 tomatillos, husks removed

2 jalapeños

3 garlic cloves

1 small onion or ½ medium onion, cut into quarters

1 cup fresh cilantro leaves

½ teaspoon Himalayan salt

Add the tomatillos, jalapeños, garlic, and onion to a dry cast-iron pan. Place the pan over medium-high heat and toast the vegetables until blackened on all sides, about 15 minutes. Transfer to a high-speed blender and add the cilantro, salt, and ½ cup water and blend until smooth. Store in a sealed container in the refrigerator for up to 1 week.

# SALSA RANCHERA

A layered, deeply flavored salsa that's more often cooked into a dish (Fideo Seco, page 24; Mixiote, page 53) than it is served on the side. (Though it is delicious enough to do so.)

MAKES ABOUT 2 CUPS

4 large tomatoes

1 small onion, cut in half

2 garlic cloves

1 slice vegan bacon, chopped

1 teaspoon fresh thyme leaves

1 teaspoon tamari soy sauce

½ teaspoon agave nectar

½ teaspoon hot sauce

½ teaspoon Himalayan salt

Add the tomatoes, onion, and garlic to a dry cast-iron pan. Place the pan over medium-high heat and toast the vegetables evenly on all sides until they start to blacken and blister, about 15 minutes. Transfer to a high-speed blender and add the bacon, thyme, tamari, agave, hot sauce, and salt. Blend until smooth. Taste and adjust the seasoning. Store in a sealed container in the refrigerator for up to 1 week.

# SALSA BRAVA

It's called "brave" for a reason—it takes fortitude to contend with this fiery salsa. You can make it exclusively green or red, but we include both tomatoes and tomatillos.

MAKES ABOUT 2 CUPS

2 Roma or plum tomatoes, whole

2 jalapeños, stemmed, halved, and seeded

1 medium tomatillo, husk removed

½ medium onion

4 garlic cloves

Juice of 1 lime

½ teaspoon Himalayan salt

Add the tomatoes, jalapeños, tomatillo, onion, and garlic to a dry cast-iron pan. Place the pan over medium-high heat and toast, turning occasionally, until the vegetables are blistered and beginning to blacken on all sides, about 20 minutes. Transfer to a high-speed blender, add the lime juice and salt, and blend to a slightly chunky consistency. Store in a sealed container in the refrigerator for up to 1 week.

# PICO DE GALLO

The simplest salsa in the game—raw, unblended, and the definition of fresh.

2 cups diced tomatoes

¾ cup diced seedless cucumber

3 tablespoons chopped fresh cilantro

1 tablespoon minced red onion

1 tablespoon fresh lemon juice

1 teaspoon seeded, minced jalapeño (or leave seeds in for more heat)

1 teaspoon Himalayan salt

In a medium bowl, add the tomatoes, cucumber, cilantro, onion, lemon juice, jalapeño, and salt and gently mix. Taste and adjust the seasoning. Store in a sealed container in the refrigerator for up to 1 week.

# PUMPKIN SEED SALSA

A chunkier, nuttier cousin of our original Salsa Verde. Great for dolloping on quesadillas.

MAKES 2¼ CUPS

2 cups Salsa Verde (page 191)

¼ cup pumpkin seeds, toasted
    until fragrant

Himalayan salt, to taste

In a high-speed blender, add the salsa verde and pumpkin seeds. Blend until smooth. Taste and adjust salt if needed. Store in a sealed container in the refrigerator for up to 1 week.

# SALSA NEGRA

You'll commonly find this salsa in the south of Mexico, and it looks just as it sounds—black. That's thanks to the generous charring that the chiles, garlic, and onion get before being blended together. But don't be mistaken—the chiles might looked cooked to oblivion, but they don't lose all their heat. If you want a salsa to bring the spicy, this is the one.

MAKES ABOUT $1\frac{1}{2}$ CUPS

25 habanero peppers

4 ounces garlic cloves (about 40 cloves)

$\frac{1}{2}$ medium onion, cut into wedges, layers separated

$\frac{1}{2}$ cup extra-virgin olive oil

3 tablespoons white vinegar

1 tablespoon Himalayan salt

Preheat the broiler. Line a baking sheet with aluminum foil.

Arrange the habaneros, garlic, and onion pieces in an even layer on the baking sheet. Broil on the rack closest to the broiler for 5 minutes. Remove from the oven and turn the vegetables as they char, then return them to the broiler. Broil until the habaneros, garlic, and onion pieces are fully blackened on all sides, 10 to 15 minutes.

Transfer to a high-speed blender and add the oil, vinegar, and salt. Blend until smooth. Store in a sealed container in the refrigerator for up to 1 week.

# SALSA MACHA

This salsa calls for frying the chiles instead of toasting them—then uses the chile-infused oil to blend all the ingredients together. The result is perfectly oily and unctuous.

MAKES ABOUT 3 CUPS

1 cup canola, rice bran, or other neutral oil

1 cup extra-virgin olive oil

2 cups dried arbol chiles (about 2 ounces)

½ cup dried morita chiles (about ¾ ounce)

15 garlic cloves

½ cup sesame seeds

¼ cup unsalted peanuts

1 tablespoon Himalayan salt

In a medium saucepan over medium heat, add and heat the canola and olive oils. Add the arbol chiles and cook briefly, until the chiles turn bright red and soften slightly, about 3 minutes. Using tongs or a slotted spoon, transfer the chiles to a large bowl. Repeat with the morita chiles and garlic cloves. Let the oil cool completely.

In a high-speed blender, add the arbol chiles, morita chiles, garlic, sesame seeds, peanuts, salt, and the cooled oil. Blend until smooth. Store in a sealed container in the refrigerator for up to 1 week.

# MOLES

Moles, or layered, deeply flavored sauces, are one of the signatures of Mexican cooking. They're basically Mexican curries, made from a complex mix of chiles and spices, with some versions including ingredients like chocolate, fruits, and nuts. The ingredients form a thick paste, which traditionally gets thinned with the cooking water of the dish you're preparing (in many cases meat, but in our case, vegetables) to transform into a silky sauce. Traditional mole recipes have often been handed down from generation to generation within families, with every household and every region having a slightly different twist. Our recipes are no different, with family recipes as the foundation, plus techniques we've picked up along the way.

# MOLE NEGRO

A classic recipe from Oaxaca using the chiles you most often find there: chilhuacle, guajillo, and pasilla. All the ingredients get roasted and toasted to deepen their flavor, which is made even more complex by anisey avocado leaf and Mexican chocolate.

MAKES ABOUT 4 CUPS

4 Roma or plum tomatoes

1 tomatillo, husk removed

¼ medium onion, layers separated

1 garlic clove

1 tablespoon almonds

1 tablespoon peanuts

2 teaspoons pumpkin seeds

2 teaspoons sesame seeds

1 small cinnamon stick

1 allspice berry

1 clove

¼ teaspoon fennel seeds

¼ teaspoon cumin seeds

1 dried avocado leaf or bay leaf

10 dried chilhuacle or cascabel chiles, seeds and veins removed and reserved

5 dried pasilla chiles, seeds and veins removed and reserved

3 dried guajillo chiles, seeds and veins removed and reserved

2½ cups vegetable broth

½ cup torn bread pieces (like ciabatta or baguette)

½ cup torn corn tortilla pieces

3 tablespoons vegan butter

2 tablespoons raisins

1 teaspoon fresh thyme leaves

1 teaspoon fresh oregano leaves (Mexican oregano if you can find it)

1 teaspoon fresh marjoram

½ disk stone-ground Mexican dark chocolate (just over ½ ounce)

1 tablespoon Himalayan salt

1 tablespoon sugar

In a large, dry cast-iron pan over medium-high heat, add the tomatoes, tomatillo, onion, and garlic. Toast them in the pan, turning occasionally, until mostly blackened on all sides, about 15 minutes. Remove from the heat and transfer the vegetables to a high-speed blender and set aside.

Wipe out any debris from the pan. Add the almonds, peanuts, pumpkin seeds, sesame seeds, cinnamon stick, allspice berry, clove, fennel seeds, and cumin seeds and arrange in a single layer. Add the avocado leaf on top. Place over very low heat and toast gently, shaking the pan occasionally, until the mixture becomes fragrant, about 5 minutes. Remove from the heat and transfer the seeds and spices to the blender and set aside.

Wipe out any debris from the pan. Add the cleaned chilhuacles, pasillas, and guajillos to the pan. Place the pan over low heat and toast the chiles for about 30 seconds per side. Remove from the heat and transfer to the blender.

Wipe out any debris from the pan. Add the reserved veins and seeds from the dried chiles. Place the pan over medium-high heat and toast until blackened and beginning to smoke, 3 to 5 minutes. Remove from the heat and transfer to the blender.

To the blender, add the vegetable broth, bread pieces, tortilla pieces, butter, raisins, thyme, oregano, and marjoram. Blend until the mixture reaches a very smooth, creamy texture.

Transfer to a large pot, place over medium-high heat, and bring to a boil. Break up the chocolate into a few pieces and add it to the pot, along with the salt and sugar. Reduce the heat to medium and stir occasionally to help the chocolate melt. Simmer until the flavors are combined, about 15 minutes. Store in a sealed container in the refrigerator for up to 1 week or in the freezer for up to 6 months.

# BLACK BEAN MOLE

While this recipe isn't traditional in concept, it's extremely traditional in spirit. We wanted to transform the side of black beans that you'd normally eat with many Mexican dishes into a deeply flavored sauce. So we took a traditional Coloradito mole—a signature Oaxacan mole—and then added black beans. The result is a satisfying mash-up between a condiment and an accompaniment.

MAKES ABOUT 4 CUPS

Canola, rice bran, or other neutral oil, for frying

1 very ripe plantain

5 tomatillos, husks removed

1 onion, quartered and layers separated

1 Roma or plum tomato

4 garlic cloves

2 teaspoons sesame seeds

1 small cinnamon stick

1 clove

¼ teaspoon cumin seeds

2 dried pasilla chiles, seeds and veins removed and reserved

1 dried New Mexico chile, seeds and veins removed and reserved

1 dried ancho chile, seeds and veins removed and reserved

1 teaspoon fresh oregano leaves (Mexican oregano if you can find it)

¼ disk stone-ground Mexican dark chocolate (just over ¼ ounce)

2 cups Black Beans (page 221)

Himalayan salt, to taste

In a Dutch oven, heavy-bottomed pot, or high-sided frying pan over medium-high heat, heat about 3 inches of oil to 350°F. Line a plate with a few layers of paper towels and place nearby for draining.

Fry the plantain, turning occasionally, until deep golden brown, 5 to 7 minutes. Transfer to the plate to drain.

In a large, dry cast-iron pan over medium-high heat, add the tomatillos, onion, tomato, and garlic. Toast them in the pan, turning occasionally, until mostly blackened on all sides, about 15 minutes. Remove from the heat and transfer to a high-speed blender and set aside.

Wipe out any debris from the pan. Add the sesame seeds, cinnamon stick, clove, and cumin seeds and arrange in a single layer. Place over very low heat and toast gently, shaking the pan occasionally, until the mixture becomes fragrant, 3 to 5 minutes. Remove from the heat, transfer to the blender, and set aside.

Wipe out any debris from the pan. Add the cleaned pasilla, New Mexico, and ancho chiles to the pan. Place the pan over low heat and toast the chiles for about 30 seconds per side. Remove from the heat and transfer the chiles to the blender.

Wipe out any debris from the pan. Add the reserved veins and seeds from the dried chiles. Place the pan over medium-high heat and toast until blackened and beginning to smoke, 3 to 5 minutes. Remove from the heat and transfer to the blender.

Add the oregano and fried plantain to the blender and blend until very smooth.

(RECIPE CONTINUES)

Pass the mixture through a fine-mesh strainer into a large pot. Place the pot over medium-high heat and bring to a boil. Reduce the heat to a strong simmer, about medium heat, and cook for 15 minutes. Break up the chocolate into a few pieces, add it to the pot, and continue simmering for 10 minutes, stirring to help the chocolate melt. Add the black beans and simmer for another 10 minutes. Season with salt to taste and add a little water if needed to thin out the mole. Store in a sealed container in the refrigerator for up to 1 week, or in the freezer for up to 6 months.

CHAPTER 8

STAPLES

# TORTILLAS

In the restaurant, we take advantage of having fresh masa (from a regenerative farm in Nebraska), as well as a team of people who know the ins and outs of making great fresh tortillas. So we get that when it comes to replicating the process at home, you want it to be restaurant-worthy in flavor, but not necessarily as complicated. For that reason, we came up with a simplified version that will deliver that still-warm-from-the-griddle product that makes a meal that much more delicious. It's a little bit more work than buying them, but the ingredients are inexpensive—as is a tortilla press, which you can find in Mexican markets or online—and the results are better than anything you can find in a store, so we encourage you to dive in at least once. But could you go to any Mexican market and buy a package of fresh corn tortillas? Absolutely.

MAKES 8 SIX-INCH TORTILLAS

2 cups masa harina (such as Maseca)

1 teaspoon Himalayan salt

1⅓ cups warm water

In a large bowl, whisk together the masa harina and salt. Slowly add the warm water and mix until mostly combined. Use your hands to gently knead and press the mixture into one large ball of dough. Let the dough rest at room temperature for 15 minutes.

Heat a dry cast-iron pan over medium-high heat until very hot.

Divide the dough into 8 equal pieces and roll each one into a tight, smooth ball between your palms. Cover the balls with a kitchen towel to keep them from drying out.

(RECIPE CONTINUES)

Line a tortilla press with two squares of parchment. (Alternatively, you could cut off the top of a quart-size zip-top plastic bag and cut down the sides to make a liner for the press.) Place a ball of dough between the parchment squares and press into a tortilla. Remove from the tortilla press and roll it to about an 8-inch diameter between the parchment or plastic.

Peel the liner away and place the raw tortilla in the hot pan. Cook for about 45 seconds. Flip and cook for about 15 more seconds, pressing down lightly with a spatula to ensure even contact with the pan. Flip once more and cook for another 15 seconds.

As you finish cooking the tortillas, stack them under a just-damp kitchen towel or in a tortilla warmer lined with a damp kitchen towel. Repeat with the remaining balls of dough.

# JACKFRUIT MIXIOTE

Jackfruit is a soft, bready fruit with a mild flavor. When cooked low and slow in a salsa ranchera–based barbecue sauce—as you would meat for a traditional mixiote—it soaks up all that flavor and takes on a shredded-meat-like texture. It's perfect for topping nachos and bowls, filling enchiladas and burritos, and putting out as part of a taco bar.

MAKES ABOUT 2 CUPS

2 tablespoons extra-virgin olive oil

1 medium onion, chopped

2 garlic cloves, minced

2 teaspoons ground cumin

½ teaspoon chipotle powder

1 (20-ounce) can jackfruit in water or brine, drained, rinsed, and broken up

½ cup Salsa Ranchera (page 192)

⅓ cup barbecue sauce

1 small dried ancho chile, toasted in a dry pan until fragrant

2 teaspoons brown sugar

¼ teaspoon Himalayan salt

In a large nonstick or cast-iron pan over medium heat, heat the oil. Add the onion, garlic, cumin, and chipotle powder and cook until the onion has softened and the spices are very fragrant, about 5 minutes. Add the jackfruit and cook, stirring occasionally, until some of the liquid from the jackfruit has cooked out, another 5 to 7 minutes.

In a high-speed blender, add the salsa ranchera, barbecue sauce, ancho chile, brown sugar, and salt and blend until smooth. Add the mixture to the jackfruit in the pan and stir to combine.

# MUSHROOM PASTOR

Mushrooms are the perfect stand-in for meat—they're dense, chewy, and take on flavor extremely well (better than meat, we'd argue). That's why when we wanted to create a plant-based version of al pastor, which is traditionally made with pork, we immediately reached for oyster mushrooms, which "pull" just like pork does after being cooked. We prepare them just as we would meat, marinating them in a toasted chile and pineapple marinade.

MAKES ABOUT 4 CUPS

1 pound oyster mushrooms, thick lower stems removed

2 dried guajillo chiles

1 dried ancho chile

1 chipotle in adobo

¼ medium onion

½ cup pineapple juice

2 tablespoons fresh orange juice

2 teaspoons apple cider vinegar

1 garlic clove

1 clove

1½ teaspoons Himalayan salt

½ teaspoon freshly ground black pepper

¼ teaspoon ground cumin

¼ teaspoon dried oregano

Over a large bowl, shred the mushrooms into bite-size pieces. Set aside.

In a large cast-iron or other heavy sauté pan over medium heat, toast the guajillo and ancho chiles until just fragrant, about 3 minutes.

In a high-speed blender, add the toasted chiles, chipotle in adobo, onion, pineapple juice, orange juice, vinegar, garlic, clove, salt, pepper, cumin, and oregano. Blend until smooth.

(RECIPE CONTINUES)

Pour the mixture over the mushrooms and toss to coat. Don't worry if the sauce doesn't look like it will coat all of the mushrooms—they'll collapse as they marinate, and you can give them another stir halfway through. Cover and marinate in the refrigerator for at least 2 hours before cooking.

When ready to serve, heat a large nonstick pan over medium heat. Using tongs or a slotted spoon, remove the mushrooms and leave any excess marinade in the bowl. Cook until the mushrooms are warmed through and the marinade has thickened a bit and become saucy, about 10 minutes.

# ESCABECHE

Go to pretty much any taquería and you'll find a bowl of lightly cooked pickled vegetables to offset the richness of the tacos, burritos, and tostadas. While our house recipe isn't exactly simple, those few extra ingredients like star anise, cumin, and cinnamon yield a pickle that is deeply flavored and satisfyingly complex.

MAKES 4 CUPS

2 teaspoons extra-virgin olive oil

1 bay leaf

1 small cinnamon stick

1 star anise

½ teaspoon cumin seeds

½ teaspoon whole black peppercorns

½ teaspoon dried thyme

½ teaspoon dried oregano

½ teaspoon red pepper flakes

½ cup sliced yellow onion, cut into ½-inch slices

1 garlic clove, smashed

2 cups apple cider vinegar

1½ teaspoons Himalayan salt

1½ teaspoons coconut sugar

4 cups mixed vegetables cut into bite-size pieces, such as baby zucchini, baby carrots, bell peppers, celery, broccoli, or cauliflower

¼ to ½ of a jalapeño, seeded and sliced into ¼-inch rounds

In a medium saucepan over medium heat, warm the oil. Add the bay leaf, cinnamon stick, star anise, cumin seeds, peppercorns, thyme, oregano, and red pepper flakes and toast in the oil until the spices are warm and fragrant, 2 minutes.

(RECIPE CONTINUES)

Add the onion and garlic and cook until the onions are slightly softened, about 3 minutes. Add the vinegar and 2 cups of water and bring to a boil. Add the salt and coconut sugar and stir to dissolve. Remove the pan from the heat and allow the mixture to cool for 5 minutes.

In a large lidded jar or covered container, add the vegetables and the jalapeño. Pour the vinegar mixture over the vegetables, adding a little more water if necessary to top off the jar and keep the vegetables submerged. Cover tightly and store in the refrigerator. The vegetables will need to pickle overnight before serving and will keep in the refrigerator for up to 2 weeks.

# RICE PAPER CHICHARRONES

Chicharrones are traditionally fried pork skins that get puffed and crispy. You can usually find them tucked into tacos, folded into stews, or scattered over a dish for extra crunch. We discovered that when you fry rice paper, it takes on an almost identical texture. And when sprinkled with salt and paprika, it becomes the perfect "crouton" for finishing off a plate.

MAKES ABOUT 3 CUPS

Canola, rice bran, or other neutral oil, for frying

12 rice paper wrappers

Himalayan salt, to taste

Paprika, for sprinkling

(RECIPE CONTINUES)

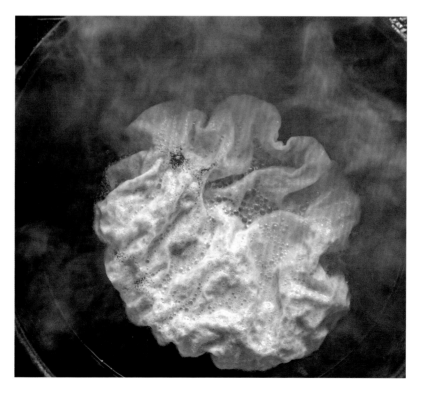

In a heavy-bottomed, high-sided frying pan over medium-high heat, heat about 1 inch of oil to 350°F. Line a plate or baking sheet with a few layers of paper towels and place nearby for draining.

Working in batches, fry the rice paper in the hot oil until it becomes puffy and crisp, about 1 minute. Transfer to the plate to drain and immediately sprinkle with a pinch of salt and paprika. Once the chicharrones have cooled slightly, break them up a bit with your hands into craggy, bite-size pieces.

# BLACK BEANS

Beans are a staple of the Mexican pantry and for good reason—they're filling, nourishing, inexpensive, and can pretty much last forever when stored correctly. There's also nothing more comforting (and delicious) than a plate of creamy, perfectly cooked beans. The secret is soaking the dried beans overnight, and then pureeing them with garlic, onion, and jalapeños until just about smooth, but not quite.

MAKES ABOUT 4 CUPS

1 cup dried black beans, soaked overnight and rinsed

1 bay leaf

½ teaspoon dried oregano

1 tablespoon extra-virgin olive oil

½ cup chopped onion

1 jalapeño, stemmed, seeded, and chopped

2 teaspoons Himalayan salt

In a medium pot over medium-high heat, add the beans, bay leaf, oregano, and just enough water to cover (about 2 cups). Bring to a boil, cover, and reduce the heat to low. Stirring occasionally, simmer until the beans are very tender, about an hour and a half.

In a medium nonstick pan over medium-high heat, heat the oil. Add the onion and jalapeño and cook, stirring occasionally, until the onions are soft and translucent, about 10 minutes.

Add the onion mixture to the pot of beans. Using an immersion blender, puree the beans until nearly smooth, keeping a little bit of texture. (Alternatively, you can carefully ladle the beans into a blender, puree them, then return them to the pot.) Add the salt and taste to adjust the seasoning.

# GREEN RICE

Rice is a familiar, comforting staple that appears in most Mexican meals. As the perfect accompaniment to our dishes, we came up with this vibrantly green version, which gets its beautiful hue, and verdant flavor, from a blend of spinach and cilantro.

MAKES ABOUT 3 CUPS

1 cup packed spinach

¼ cup packed fresh cilantro

1 teaspoon Himalayan salt

1 tablespoon extra-virgin olive oil

½ cup chopped yellow onion

2 garlic cloves, chopped

1 cup basmati rice

In a high-speed blender, add the spinach, cilantro, salt, and 1¾ cups of water and blend until smooth.

In a medium saucepan over medium heat, heat the oil. Add the onion and garlic and cook, stirring occasionally, until the onions start to look translucent, about 5 minutes. Add the rice and the blended spinach mixture and stir to combine. Increase the heat to high and bring to a boil. Cover, reduce the heat to low, and simmer until the water has been absorbed, 15 to 20 minutes. Remove from the heat, leaving the lid on to steam for an additional 5 minutes. Fluff with a fork and keep covered until serving.

# COCONUT BACON

These crispy, smoky bits are all over our menu because they're not only the perfect meaty substitute, but they also lend great depth of flavor and texture to just about any dish. We highly recommend keeping a batch on hand to sprinkle in salads, bowls, tacos, and pretty much anything else in a tortilla.

MAKES 4 CUPS

4 cups dried coconut chips

2 tablespoons extra-virgin
    olive oil, plus more for the pan

2 teaspoons chipotle powder

$1\frac{1}{4}$ teaspoons Himalayan salt

$\frac{3}{4}$ cup maple syrup

Preheat the oven to 250°F.

In a wide, heavy-bottomed pot over medium-high heat, add the coconut chips, oil, chipotle powder, and salt. Toast for 10 minutes, stirring continuously so the chips do not burn. When the coconut chips are a dark golden color, stir in the maple syrup and continue cooking until the chips are well coated, another 2 minutes.

Transfer the coconut chips to an oiled baking sheet and toast them in the oven until they are crispy, 10 to 12 minutes. Check in every 3 or 4 minutes and turn the chips over to make sure they cook evenly.

When the coconut chips are dry and crisp, remove them from the oven and allow them to cool completely. The coconut bacon can be stored in an airtight container or glass jar for up to 1 month outside of the refrigerator.

CHAPTER 9

# BEBIDAS

# AGUAS FRESCAS

In the farmers markets and on the streets of Mexico, you often find vendors with jugs full of agua fresca, or "fresh water." It's decidedly delicious and refreshing and is typically nothing more than water that's been flavored with a splash of strained fresh fruit juice plus a sweetener. For our versions, we've blended cucumber, watermelon, and orange with the fresh notes of basil, mint, and rosemary, plus gentle sweeteners like agave nectar and coconut sugar. And then there's our hoja santa agua fresca, using the leaf of the same name, which has a unique root beer–like flavor.

## HOJA SANTA AGUA FRESCA

MAKES 6 CUPS (SERVES 6)

1 fresh hoja santa leaf

½ cup fresh lemon juice

½ cup fresh lime juice

½ cup agave nectar

¼ cup chia seeds

In a high-speed blender, add the hoja santa leaf and 2 cups of water. Blend until the hoja santa is thoroughly broken down. Pour the mixture through a fine-mesh strainer into a pitcher. Add the lemon juice, lime juice, agave, chia seeds, and 2 more cups of water and stir. Chill for at least 2 hours to allow the chia seeds to expand. Serve chilled.

## CUCUMBER LIME AGUA FRESCA

MAKES 8 CUPS (SERVES 8)

4 Persian cucumbers, ends trimmed

1 cup lightly packed fresh mint leaves

¾ cup fresh lime juice

½ cup coconut sugar

In a high-speed blender, add the cucumbers, mint, lime juice, sugar, and 1 cup of water and blend until very smooth. Pour the mixture through a fine-mesh strainer set over a pitcher. Add 5 cups of cold water and stir. Serve over ice.

## ORANGE AGUA FRESCA

MAKES ABOUT 6 CUPS (SERVES 6)

1 cup fresh orange juice

1 cup strawberries, hulled

1 sprig fresh rosemary

2 tablespoons agave nectar

In a pitcher, add the orange juice, strawberries, and rosemary. Let sit at room temperature for 30 minutes to infuse. Add the agave and 4 cups of cold water and stir to combine. Serve over ice.

## WATERMELON AGUA FRESCA

MAKES ABOUT 8 CUPS (SERVES 8)

6 cups seedless watermelon (from about ½ watermelon)

½ cup fresh cranberries

½ cup packed fresh basil leaves

2 tablespoons agave nectar

In a high-speed blender, add the watermelon, cranberries, basil, and a small splash of water. Blend until smooth. Pour the mixture through a fine-mesh strainer set over a pitcher. Add the agave and 4 cups of cold water and stir. Taste and add more agave if desired. Serve over ice.

# CHAMOYADA

Chamoy is a Mexican condiment that's unparalleled in flavor by anything we've come across. Thanks to its unique combination of dried or preserved fruit, lime juice, and chiles, it manages to be sweet, sour, salty, and spicy all at once. The recipe here will yield more than you'll need, so when you're not using it as the base for this mango smoothie that you'll commonly find on the streets of Mexico City, you can drizzle it over fresh fruit, as it's also often enjoyed.

SERVES 4

## FOR THE CHAMOY

$2/3$ cup cranberries, fresh or frozen and thawed

$1/3$ cup apricot jam

$1/3$ cup fresh lemon juice

$1/2$ teaspoon Himalayan salt

$1/2$ teaspoon chipotle powder

## FOR THE CHAMOYADA

4 cups mango puree

4 cups ice

$1/2$ cup sugar

3 tablespoons fresh lime juice

1 teaspoon Himalayan salt

**Make the chamoy:** In a high-speed blender, add the cranberries, apricot jam, lemon juice, salt, and chipotle powder with $2/3$ cup of water. Blend until nearly smooth, keeping a bit of texture. Taste for seasoning and add more salt and chipotle if needed.

**Make the chamoyada:** In a high-speed blender, add the mango puree, ice, sugar, lime juice, and salt and blend until smooth. The mixture should have the consistency of a smoothie.

Dip the rims of four glasses in the chamoy. Divide the mango mixture among the glasses and add a little more chamoy on top.

# HORCHATA

This is one of the original plant-based foods of Mexico, a thick, sweet, milkshake-like drink made with rice as the base and spiced with cinnamon and vanilla.

MAKES ABOUT 6 CUPS (SERVES 6)

1 cup basmati rice

2 cinnamon sticks

1½ cups unsweetened almond milk

¼ cup plus 1 tablespoon agave nectar

1 tablespoon vanilla extract

Rinse the rice thoroughly to remove any excess starch. Drain and add to a large jar, along with the cinnamon sticks and 4 cups of water. Cover and let soak overnight in the refrigerator.

Transfer the rice mixture to a high-speed blender and blend until it's as smooth and milky as possible, and the cinnamon has been finely ground. This will probably take a few minutes.

Fold a large cheesecloth into at least 4 layers and place it over a fine-mesh strainer set over a large bowl. Slowly pour the rice mixture to strain out any solids and excess starches, pausing to let the liquid work its way through when needed.

Transfer the strained liquid to a pitcher and add the almond milk, agave, and vanilla. Whisk to combine. Chill for at least 2 hours and taste for sweetness, adding more agave if needed.

# PURISTA

We knew we had to bring it when it came to our house margarita, so we came up with a version that's every bit as clean and focused as our food. We took a page from Julio Bermejo's playbook, since he's the person to credit for bringing fresh, seasonal ingredients into West Coast bartending and reinventing the margarita, making it with agave instead of the simple syrup version that became popular in the '90s at Tommy's Mexican Restaurant in San Francisco. Then we stripped things down, resulting in a spirit-forward (read: strong) cocktail that's still refreshingly balanced with hints of lime juice, agave, and orange bitters.

MAKES 2 COCKTAILS

### FOR THE CHILE SALT (MAKES ABOUT $^1/_2$ CUP)

½ cup Himalayan salt

2 teaspoons chipotle powder

### FOR THE AGAVE SYRUP (MAKES 1 CUP)

⅔ cup agave nectar

⅓ cup boiling water

### FOR THE COCKTAILS

4 ounces blanco tequila or mezcal

2 ounces fresh lime juice

4 dashes orange bitters

Lime peel or jalapeño slice, for the rim

**Make the chile salt:** In a small jar, add the salt and chipotle powder. Store covered for up to 1 month.

**Make the agave syrup:** In a medium jar, add the agave and water and stir until the agave has dissolved into the water. Cover and store in the refrigerator for up to 1 month.

(RECIPE CONTINUES)

**Make the cocktails:** In a cocktail shaker with ice, add the tequila, lime juice, ¾ ounce of the agave syrup, and the bitters. Shake well.

Dip two rocks glasses in the chile salt and add ice. Strain the tequila mixture over the ice and garnish with a lime peel.

# SO FRESA SO CLEAN

This was one of our first cocktails on the menu, and it lives up to its name—fresh and clean. It's been a staple ever since, namely because a strawberry-rosewater tequila sour is the perfect drinking companion for our food, but also because sours are typically made with egg whites, making them off-limits to our plant-based guests. We, on the other hand, make ours using aquafaba, or the liquid that remains after cooking or soaking chickpeas. It's virtually taste-free, and when whipped, it gets delightfully frothy.

MAKES 2 COCKTAILS

## FOR THE STRAWBERRY–ROSEWATER SYRUP (MAKES ABOUT 1$^1$/$_2$ CUPS)

10 strawberries, hulled

1 cup sugar

4 drops rosewater

## FOR THE COCKTAILS

1½ ounces blanco tequila

2 ounces fresh lemon juice

2 ounces aquafaba (liquid from cooked chickpeas, can use canned)

1 ounce strawberry brandy

2 rose petals, for garnish (optional)

**Make the syrup:** In a high-speed blender, add the strawberries, sugar, and rosewater and blend until smooth. Pass the mixture through a fine-mesh strainer into a medium jar and store, covered, in the refrigerator for up to 1 week.

**Make the cocktails:** In a cocktail shaker without ice, add the tequila, lemon juice, aquafaba, brandy, and 1 ounce of the strawberry-rosewater syrup. Shake vigorously for 2 minutes to froth the aquafaba. Add ice and shake again for 1 minute. Strain into two rocks glasses with ice. Garnish with the rose petals, if using.

# TEQUILA PALOMA

The roots of a paloma are charmingly humble (it's typically tequila and Squirt citrus soda with a squeeze of lime and a pinch of salt), so we wanted to honor that playfulness while giving things a more polished and updated twist. The result: a punchy sorbet-based cocktail with bright citrus flavor. While it's not exactly the simplest cocktail to make, the sorbet and grapefruit-infused liquor keep well and yield a number of drinks. And once they're prepared, a paloma is only minutes away. Though, if you were inclined, you could also substitute 1½ ounces grapefruit juice for the sorbet.

MAKES 2 COCKTAILS

## FOR THE GRAPEFRUIT PONCHE SORBET (MAKES ABOUT 1 CUP)

1 cup fresh grapefruit juice

2½ tablespoons Ponche Pajarote Grapefruit and Rosemary Liqueur

## FOR THE GRAPEFRUIT–INFUSED COCCHI AMERICANO (MAKES 1 CUP)

1 cup Cocchi Americano

Peel from 1 grapefruit

## FOR THE COCKTAILS

4 ounces blanco tequila

1½ ounces pamplemousse liqueur

1½ ounces fresh lime juice

Himalayan salt, for the rim

3 ounces grapefruit soda

1 slice fresh grapefruit, halved, for garnish (optional)

**Make the sorbet:** In the bowl of an ice-cream maker, add the grapefruit juice and the Pajarote. Let the mixture circulate until frozen, about 8 minutes. Transfer to a covered storage container and store in the freezer.

**Make the infused Cocchi Americano:** In a small bowl, add the Cocchi Americano and the grapefruit peels. Stir gently to agitate and let sit for 30 minutes. Pass the mixture through a fine-mesh strainer to remove any pith or debris, store in an airtight jar or bottle, and refrigerate.

**Make the cocktails:** In a cocktail shaker with ice, add the tequila, pamplemousse liqueur, lime juice, and ¾ ounce each of the sorbet and the grapefruit-infused Cocchi Americano. Shake for 1 minute. Rim two collins glasses with the salt and add ice. Add the grapefruit soda to the shaker and strain the mixture over the ice. Garnish with the grapefruit, if using.

SUFFERING MADRE

# SUFFERING MADRE

There's a classic tiki cocktail called the suffering bastard, which is what a bartender would whip up if a particularly hungover patron pulled up a stool. We wanted to put our stamp on the hair of the dog, so we updated the original whiskey-based recipe to include agave spirits, more specifically a coconut-washed añejo, or aged tequila. Then we added ginger and turmeric for some botanical healing.

MAKES 2 COCKTAILS

### FOR THE GINGER–TURMERIC SYRUP

12 ounces fresh turmeric root

½ cup fresh carrot juice

½ cup ginger juice

1½ cups sugar

### FOR THE COCKTAIL

4 ounces Coconut-Washed Añejo (recipe follows)

1½ ounces fresh lime juice

4 dashes mole bitters

3 ounces club soda

2 sprigs fresh mint, for garnish

**Make the syrup:** Using a juicer, juice the turmeric. Alternatively, you can grate the turmeric, place it in cheesecloth or a nut-milk bag, and squeeze out the juice, discarding the pulp.

In a high-speed blender, add the turmeric juice, carrot juice, ginger juice, and sugar. Blend until the sugar has dissolved into the juices. Store refrigerated in an airtight container for up to 1 week.

**Make the cocktail:** In a cocktail shaker with ice, add the añejo, 1 ounce of the ginger-turmeric syrup, the lime juice, and bitters. Shake for 1 minute. Add the soda and strain into two collins glasses with ice. Garnish with the mint.

# COCONUT-WASHED AÑEJO

Añejo is an oak-aged tequila that takes on rich, deep, almost vanilla-flecked notes. It's smoother than young tequila and extremely sippable. We like to "wash" this spirit with virgin coconut oil, which gives it an even silkier mouthfeel plus a tasty coconut flavor. That's a big bonus in the cocktail-making department because coconut milk tends to separate and settle when used as the base of a drink. You can sub this into just about any recipe; we highly recommend it for tequila old-fashioneds.

MAKES 1 CUP

1 cup añejo tequila

¼ cup virgin coconut oil, melted

In a wide-mouth jar, add the tequila and oil and stir. Cover and let sit at room temperature for 8 hours. Place the jar in the freezer for 4 more hours, or until the coconut oil has frozen into one piece. Remove the frozen oil and pour the tequila through a fine-mesh strainer into a jar or bottle. Store covered at room temperature.

# SPECIAL MENUS

# *CINCO DE MAYO

Guacamole

Esquites

Nachos al Pastor

Gorditas

Churros

Purista

# *DINNER WITH FRIENDS

Tostadas al Ajillo

Tostadas al Jackfruit Mixiote

Esquites

Coliflor Frito

Fudge Brownies with Salted Mezcal

Caramel Sauce and Cashew Whipped Cream

So Fresa So Clean

# *MOTHER'S DAY

Plantain Molotes with Mole Negro

Flautas de Hibiscus

Uchepos

Chiles Rellenos

Tiramisu con Mezcal

Horchata

# *BIRTHDAY NIGHT

Mexican-Style Street Corn

Calabaza and Onion Quesadillas

Chimichangas

Black Bean Burgers

Coffee Flan

Suffering Madre

# *NEW YEAR'S EVE

Crema de Elote

Fideo Seco

Pozole

Mushroom Fajitas

Pineapple Upside-Down Cake

Paloma

# *BRUNCH

Madre Coconut Ceviche

Chilaquiles

Mango Sopes

Chamoyada

# *LATE-NIGHT MUNCHIES

Repollitos Fritos

Empanadas

Tlayudas

Al Pastor Madre Tacos

Mexican Wedding Cookies

Mexican Chocolate Ice Cream

# Acknowledgments

It is our pleasure to acknowledge so many talented people who have made this book possible:

The Engelhart family—Matthew, Terces, Ryland, and Cary—the creators of Gracias Madre, for taking the leap of faith to open this restaurant and being the best partners ever.

Founding chef Chandra Gilbert, whose incredible culinary talent and leadership launched the nation's most successful plant-based restaurant.

Chef Alan Sánchez, who brought a unique and creative palate to the Gracias Madre menu, which continues to honor Mexican culinary traditions while being firmly rooted in the vibrant food landscape of Southern California.

Community has always been a hallmark of the Gracias Madre experience, and our success is due in no small part to the Heart of the House team in each of our restaurants. We would like to thank these hard-working individuals for their contribution, and in particular:

Miguel Gutierrez, our one-of-a-kind, world-class kitchen manager at Gracias Madre West Hollywood, for his dedicated leadership over many years.

Charlie D'Armetta, our general manager, for making the magic happen with the food, experience, and ambiance, and for being a true leader. And Mimi Chong, for supporting this mission every day.

Maxwell Reis, for always innovating our spirits and beverage program and taking our guests on an unparalleled educational adventure through the world of agave.

Patrick Hotchkiss, our director of operations, for being a true advocate for the Gracias Madre brand and elevating our service at every level. Thanks to you, we've spread the Gracias Madre love to Newport Beach.

Scott Burnham, for being so persistent about bringing Gracias Madre to Newport and for holding the high bar for attention to detail and design.

Mark Lehman, our brilliant attorney and wise consigliere, and Chris Bonbright, our managing partner, for putting it all together and setting us up to succeed.

This book would not have come together as smoothly and seamlessly without Chef Seizan Dreux Ellis. Thank you for the creativity and conviction of spirit that you bring to everything you do, and for all the ways you supported this project.

Heartfelt thanks to Lisa Romerein, Rebecca Farr, and Robin Turk, for their beautiful styling and photography, which perfectly capture the creativity and vibrancy of our menu.

We wish to express our thanks to TableArt, one of our favorite boutiques in Los Angeles, and its owner, Walter Lowry. TableArt loaned us many pieces for this book, including dinnerware by small, difficult-to-find producers such as Christiane Perrochon, Potomak Studio, DBO Home, Jan Burtz, and Haand, to name just a few. We are grateful for their participation in this project and encourage our community to seek out and support their many artists at tableartonline.com.

We would also like to highlight the awe-inspiring work by two ceramicists who supported this project with beautiful custom pieces exclusively for the book: Emily Brown of Ojai, California (emilybrownceramics.com), and Kari Ytterdal of Kari Ceramics in Amsterdam (kariceramics.com).

Thank you to our publishing team:

Nicole Tourtelot, our literary agent, for always leading the way with fierce grace.

Lucia Watson, our editor, for giving this book shape and purpose, and Suzy Swartz for capably ensuring its successful entry into the world.

We are also so grateful for our writer Rachel Holtzman, who has crafted a book that not only traces the birth and development of Gracias Madre but also manages to honor all of the cross-cultural influences that have defined it over the years.

JACKFRUIT

# INDEX

Note: Page numbers in *italics* indicate photos separate from recipes.